SEX-ROLE ISSUES IN MENTAL HEALTH

Kay F. Schaffer
The University of Toledo

ADDISON-WESLEY
PUBLISHING COMPANY

Reading, Massachusetts
Menlo Park, California
London • Amsterdam
Don Mills, Ontario • Sydney

This book is in the
ADDISON-WESLEY SERIES IN CLINICAL AND PROFESSIONAL PSYCHOLOGY

Leonard D. Goodstein
Series Editor

 Printed in the United States of America. Published simultaneously in Canada. Library of Congress Catalog Card No. 79-53872.

ISBN 0-201-06762-5
ABCDEFGHIJ-DO-89876543210

For my mother,
Wenonah L. Frankforther

Foreword

Clinical psychology is a rapidly expanding area of inquiry and practice. Traditional lines between clinical and the other subdisciplines of psychology are rapidly eroding. Research in information processing has direct impact upon behavior therapy, work in physiological psychology affects our work in biofeedback, community psychologists need to keep abreast of what is happening in social psychology, and so on. At the same time, clinical psychologists are being called on to work in a variety of new settings, and to continually develop new skills as well as to utilize their existing skills. Health Maintenance Organizations (HMOs) ask clinical psychologists not only to provide direct clinical service to clients but also to help change the health-related behaviors of clients who do not require direct service. Community mental health centers ask their clinicians to provide direct service and to assist in developing prevention programs and program evaluation procedures. These are but a few examples of how the field of clinical psychology is expanding.

It is difficult for the professional practitioner as well as the student of clinical psychology to keep in touch with what is happening in the field. Traditional textbooks can give only superficial coverage to these recent changes and the journal literature does not provide a broad overview. The Addison-Wesley Series in Clinical and Professional Psychology is an effort to fill this gap. Taken as a whole, the series could be used as an introduction to the field of clinical psychology. A subset of these books, such as those on therapy, for example, could serve as a text for a course in therapy. Single volumes can be used for seminars when supplemented by journal articles, or as supplemental texts for courses in which the instructor feels the text is lacking in coverage of that area, or for short courses for the active professional. We hope that each of these volumes, written or edited by experts in the area, will also serve as an up-to-date overview of that area for the interested professional who feels the need of updating.

One of the most important characteristics of contemporary professional psychology is a heightened awareness of the issues involved in working across gender, racial, socioeconomic, and other lines. Such differences require thoughtfulness and concern by both consumers and providers of professional services. In this volume the author has provided an introduction to the expanding field of sex-role differences as these differences affect the delivery of mental-health services.

Webster defines a *Primer* as "a small introductory volume on a subject." It is hoped that this volume will serve such a function in the area of sex roles and mental health.

Leonard D. Goodstein

Preface

During recent years there has been intense interest in the effects of stereotyped sex roles on the behavior and attitudes of American women and men. Literature and research based entirely on the behavior and attitudes of men are being supplemented and replaced by data based on both women and men. As a consequence, more people are becoming aware of the differences in the roles that our society prescribes for the two sexes and of other limitations and pressures that stereotyped sex roles place on all members of our society.

It is especially important that educators, service providers, and students in professional fields that are related to mental health become aware of the influences of sex roles on their own lives and on the lives of other people. Professionals in mental-health fields, as well as people in general, are affected by their own values and attitudes about sex roles, and their beliefs about sex-appropriate behaviors can often affect the services they provide to both men and women.

This book is designed for use in psychology courses that deal with sex-role issues and mental-health issues for women and men, and it is also relevant for similar courses in sociology, social work, women's studies, and other related fields. It is also designed to be useful for professionals who are already working as service providers and educators.

The first three chapters of the book focus on sex differences and sex-role influences during childhood, adolescence, and adulthood and on the apparent changes that are occurring in attitudes and behavior as a result of an increasing awareness of the effects of stereotyped sex roles. Chapters 4 and 5 emphasize the effects of sex roles and sex biases in the areas of intelligence, achievement, and career development for women and men, and the effects of test bias are examined and discussed. In Chapters 6 and 7, the influences of marriage and other interpersonal relationships on mental health are emphasized, and the focus is on the various methods and consequences of psychotherapy for both women and men. In the last chapter, sex-role issues are discussed in relation to racial and social class issues, and the concept of therapist power is examined.

The main goal of the book is to increase the reader's awareness of sex-role influences on the mental health of women and men within our society. Several case study examples are included throughout the text to assist the reader in assessing his or her own attitudes and sex-related biases about various men and women clients, and suggestions for providing nonsexist services for clients are also included within each chapter.

Toledo, Ohio
July 1979

K. F. S.

Contents

1

Sex Differences and Sex Roles

2

Sex-Role Socialization Outside of the Family

3 Awareness and Change

4 Intelligence and Achievement

5 Career Choice and Career Counseling

6

Marriage and Mental Health

7

Psychotherapy

8

Sex Roles and Social Issues

1

Sex Differences and Sex Roles

Overview

Throughout history, in every society, people have been intensely interested in the differences between women and men. It has been generally assumed that the sexes differ not only in basic anatomy, but also in temperament, personality, ability, and virtually every other human characteristic. It has been supposed that men and women do not think in the same way, do not hold the same values, do not desire the same things out of life, and do not share equally the power, status, and privileges within the same society. Every society has created barriers between the sexes by distinguishing separate behavior roles for men and for women.

During recent years, researchers have begun to take a new look at the study of sex differences and the influences that these assumed differences have on people's lives. Although no one doubts that some basic, obvious physical and reproductive differences do exist between women and men, it is increasingly apparent that many of the differences that have been presumed to exist simply do not stand up under careful analysis. Yet, individuals often unknowingly accept these assumed differences, allow them to shape their lives, and then transmit their beliefs to their children, thus perpetuating the cycle.

Since misconceptions about expected differences between men and women tend to affect most people within a society, professionals in mental-health fields are not immune from these influences, even though they may be aware of the research and literature on sex differences. The conscious and unconscious beliefs, values, and stereotypes about sex differences and sex roles that the mental-health professional endorses will affect the appropriateness and quality of the service he or she brings to clients as well as the potential effectiveness of these services within a rapidly changing society.

Before turning our attention to some examples of sex-role influences, let us briefly define the important terms that will be discussed throughout the text.

Definition of Terms

The primary category for the classification of humans is their sex, and on the basis of their physical sex characteristics, babies are labeled "male" or "female." *Sex differences* are established biological differences between the sexes, such as reproductive differences and physical differences. Although other types of behavior demonstrated by men and women within a given society may differ considerably, except for aggression, mathematical ability, and visual-spatial ability in men and verbal ability in women, there is no conclusive evidence to indicate that these differences in behavior are caused by biological or hormonal factors (Maccoby and Jacklin, 1974).

Gender identity is an aspect of self-concept and personality and refers to the awareness of belonging to one of the two sexes (Stoller, 1968). Gender identity usually becomes obvious around age two when a child knows she is a girl or he is a boy, and it becomes more complex as the child develops. Gender identity is encouraged from birth when the child is immediately wrapped in a pink or a blue blanket or may be clothed in a hot pink or baby blue gown that proclaims, "I was born at Toledo Hospital."

The awareness of gender opens the way to the understanding of *gender roles,* which are the observable behavior a person displays to other people in society in order to indicate his or her gender (Stoller, 1968). Since other people validate our self-perceptions, their reactions are very important, and if they are not reinforcing, a person's gender identity may be confused. A parent who, for example, is mentally ill or mentally retarded, and who dresses a male child as a girl and reinforces him only for behavior considered appropriate for girls, can undermine the boy's self-concept as "masculine" and cause him to develop a confused or shifting gender identity. If the inappropriate reinforcement continues until or beyond age three, gender identity becomes almost impossible to change or correct (Money and Ehrhardt, 1972).

Sex roles are cultural expectations concerning the appropriate behavior of males and females. Although cultures vary according to the specific tasks and traits they expect of men and women, most prescribe different characteristics and behaviors that are supposed to be associated with the members of each sex. Our sex roles are greatly influenced by our physical identity as male or female. Both biological and cultural influences are involved in determining the appropriate sex roles within a given society. For example, the "core" elements of the female role in the United States currently include: (1) a concentration on marriage, home, and children as the primary focus; (2) a reliance on a male provider for sustenance and status symbolized by taking the husband's name and sharing his income; (3) an expectation that women will emphasize nurturance and life-preserving activities both literally (creating life) and symbolically (taking care of the helpless); (4) a stress on beauty; and (5) a ban on the direct expression of aggression, assertion, and power striving (Keller, 1974). The prescribed male sex role, on the other hand, includes: (1) physical strength and accomplishment; (2) emotional control and alienation from feelings (except for anger); (3) strong bonds with others, but avoidance of emotional intimacy with same-sex others; and (4) provision of sustenance and protection for women and children (Pleck, 1976).

These sex roles tend to be confining and limiting for both women and men, and at the present time, especially for women, are in the process of widening and changing. The intense interest in female sex roles is also reflected in some complementary changes that are beginning to occur in sex roles for men.

Stereotypes are consensual beliefs and assumptions about the characteristics and personality traits of men and women. Sex-role stereotypes often do not make allowances for individual differences within the sexes. Based on an individual's physical identity as male or female, people will frequently make assumptions about that individual without having any other information. Society tends to emphasize group differences and to ignore evidence that does not support existing stereotypes. Stereotypes sometimes develop based on the observation of real differences between groups—for example, that men are predisposed to be more aggressive than women—and then these differences become exaggerated beyond the original evidence. Other stereotypes appear to have been false and inaccurate from inception and to have no basis of underlying truth. An example of such a stereotype is the notion that has persisted throughout history that men as a group are superior to women as a group in intelligence even though this is not and never has been the case. When stereotypes limit the potential of some members of society, they can be damaging and destructive to all members of that society.

Sex-Role Stereotypes in Operation

Many mental-health professionals and other social scientists, as well as the general public, long believed that it was crucial for the personal adjustment and happiness of the individual that he or she learn and identify with appropriate sex roles and stereotypes. In the last few years, however, people have begun to question the positive value of prescribed sex roles and to express concern about their possible detrimental effects on both men and women. Still, as of this date, sex-role stereotypes are very pervasive in our society, not only within the general population, but within the mental-health professions as well.

Biases within Society in General

In 1968, a group of investigators (Rosenkrantz et al.) developed a sex-role questionnaire that has been widely used to examine the sex-role stereotypes held by American women and men. In the initial study of the series, the questionnaire was presented to college students who were asked to rate adult men, adult women, and themselves on a large number of bipolar characteristics. These characteristics were rated on a scale from 1 to 7 and included traits such as aggression ("not at all aggressive—"very aggressive") and emotion ("not at all emotional"—"very emotional") that were thought to differentiate men and women. The results of this early study indicated that the college students of both sexes agreed to a significant degree about the differences in behavior that men and women should be expected to exhibit. Men were typically rated higher than women on such characteristics as aggression, objectivity, independence, competition, and ambition, while women were consistently rated higher on such characteristics as passivity, dependency, emotionality, and submissiveness.

Following the development of the Rosenkrantz sex-role questionnaire, the results from numerous studies of sex-role stereotypes have indicated that men and women in our society have different, well-articulated concepts of "male" and "female" and that the characteristics attributed to men are more positive and socially desirable than those attributed to women.

A few years later, Broverman et al. (1972) conducted an extensive series of investigations examining the sex-role stereotypes we hold. They concluded that despite apparent changes in sex-role definitions in contemporary society in recent decades, stereotypic thinking about sex roles is still pervasive and persistent. American men and women assign different personality traits to women and men, and these differences exist across groups which differ in age, sex, marital status, religion, and educational level. Characteristics assigned to men form a cluster of related behaviors, including competence, rationality, and assertiveness. A greater number of desirable traits are assigned to men than to women. Men are consistently described as more aggressive, independent, dominant, active, competitive, and self-confident than women. Women are consistently described as more gentle, sensitive, emotional, expressive, neat, and tactful than men. The valued traits for women form a cluster reflecting warmth and expressiveness.

Broverman et al. also concluded that these sex-role stereotypes are incorporated into the self-concepts of both women and men and that they are often uncritically accepted and even considered desirable. This does not always work to the advantage of women. In a highly competitive society such as ours, assertiveness and competence—so-called "male" traits—are more highly valued than warmth and expressiveness. Nevertheless, women as well as men endorsed the prevailing stereotypes. Women also incorporated the more negative aspects of the feminine stereotypes into their self-concepts, including the traits of relative incompetence, irrationality, and passivity. Furthermore, the investigators concluded that not only are members of each sex expected to have traits appropriate for their assigned sex role, they are also expected not to exhibit traits assigned to the other sex. Roles are mutually exclusive for many important psychological traits.

In another study investigating the effects of sex-role stereotypes, Goldberg (1968) asked female college students to evaluate articles on the following topics: law, city planning, linguistics, art history, education, and dietetics. For each article, half the subjects saw a male author's name and half saw a female author's name. Articles on *all* topics were evaluated more favorably when the students thought they had been written by men, thus Goldberg concluded that women believe in existing stereotypes and are, consequently, prejudiced against other women. We should point out, however, that several recent attempts to replicate Goldberg's findings have produced no evidence of female bias against women, and the results of one study indicated a profemale bias on the part of both male and female subjects (Hough and Allen, 1975). It is difficult to determine how much of this represents a genuine change in attitude as opposed to a desire to express fashionable ideas, but Hough and Allen found that the profemale bias disappeared when subjects believed they were hooked up to a lie-detector apparatus.

In another related study (Lao et al., 1975) over 600 male and female undergraduate students rated male and female role players on intelligence and likability. Participating students viewed videotapes in which two men and two women in turn played high, medium, and low assertive roles. Role players were equated for age, physical attractiveness, and general intelligence. The results indicated that male players were judged to be more intelligent than female players in every condition. While medium assertiveness was associated with the highest level of perceived intelligence for both sexes, high assertiveness resulted in lower ratings of intelligence for women but in higher ratings of intelligence for men. The men were also rated as more likable than the women, and high assertiveness in women had a much more negative effect than high assertiveness in men. These college-student subjects, people who are sometimes considered liberal and fairly open-minded toward variation in sex-role behavior, indicated that they believed that men are in general more intelligent and likable than women.

Garske (1975) also investigated sex-role stereotypes using college students. In his study, undergraduate volunteers rated hypothetical "stimulus persons" using sex-role stereotype questionnaires. The stimulus people included "adult male" and "adult female," "male" and "female" undergraduate students, and "male" and "female" graduate students. Consistent with previous research, the adult stimulus persons were described in stereotypic sex-role terms. The male and female undergraduates were also rated according to the stereotypes, but these ratings were less extreme than those elicited by the adults. The male graduate student was seen as having sex-role characteristics similar to those of the undergraduates, while the female graduate student was seen as significantly more masculine, with attributes similar to those ascribed to the adult male. In this study, college students still endorsed existing stereotypes when presented with adult stimulus persons, but they modified these stereotypes when confronted with other stimulus people. Biased attitudes were still apparent, but variations of role information did alter the results significantly.

Biases within the Mental-Health Field

Sex-role biases appear to be pervasive in our society. Since people in general hold strong beliefs about what constitutes sex-appropriate behavior, it is only logical to assume that many psychologists, psychiatrists, social workers, and other educators and mental-health professionals also share these beliefs. In deciding whom to treat, what treatment goals to establish, and which techniques to use, mental-health professionals must exercise value judgments and make decisions about what is to be considered "appropriate" behavior. Whenever treatment or counseling goals for an individual depend upon his or her sex, race, age, or social class, biases are evident. Bias becomes prejudice when the biased person is resistant to information that might lead to a changed belief (Schlossberg and Pietrofesa, 1978).

The single most important study on sex biases in the mental-health field was conducted by Broverman et al. in 1970. It was so important not only because it was one of the first studies of this topic, but also because of the wide coverage it received both in the mental-health professions and in the popular press. Broverman et al. asked both male and female practicing clinicians to rate men and women using the Rosenkrantz sex-role questionnaire. The clinicians were divided into three groups. The first group was asked to rate a mature, healthy, competent male; the second group to rate a mature, healthy, competent female; and the third group to rate a mature, healthy, competent adult. There were no differences between male and female clinicians in their ratings, and they strongly agreed as to what characteristics define mental health for men and women. Healthy men and healthy adults were described in very similar terms, but healthy women and healthy adults were not described in the same way. Healthy men and adults were assigned positive characteristics, such as independence, objectivity, and competence, significantly more often than healthy women; and both the male and female clinicians indicated that healthy women are more submissive, less independent, more easily influenced, less competitive, more emotional, and less objective than healthy men and healthy adults. The investigators concluded that there is apparently a double standard of mental health for men and for women and that the descriptions assigned to "healthy" women are not considered healthy for men or for adults in general.

In a related study, male and female counselors were asked to evaluate mental health based on case studies in which the client was identically described except for the name, Joan or John, and political orientation, right or left. Both male and female clinicians described the politically left-involved female as having more emotional maladjustment than any other subject, male or female (Abramowitz et al., 1973).

Both of these studies, which have been widely interpreted as demonstrating sex biases, especially against women, have been criticized for problems in research design and presentation of data, as well as for the tendencies of the investigators to go beyond the data and make "simplistic conclusions about sex bias not likely to be helpful to our overall understanding" (Stricker, 1977).

More recent studies (Maxfield, 1976; Oppedisano-Reich, 1976) have not supported the conclusions that mental-health stereotypes are indicative of a double standard of health with an overall bias against women. Instead, they have concluded that on an *individual* basis the sex of the therapist and the sex of the patient may make a significant difference. In addition, in some interactions involving sex, there may be biases toward rather than against women. The results of these recent studies may be reflecting a verbal awareness of sex-role issues. At the same time, conclusions cannot be made about the behavior of clinicians with male and female clients, even though their levels of conscious awareness of potential biases, especially against women, are apparently changing.

APA Task Force on Sex Bias

The American Psychological Association established a task force to investigate the effects on women of sex biases in therapeutic practice. The task force method was to survey female psychologists as both consumers and practitioners of psychotherapy to determine what they considered to be sexism in therapy.

The Report of the Task Force on Sex Bias and Sex-Role Stereotyping in Psychotherapeutic Practices (1975) indicated that four general areas of bias and stereotyping emerged from the survey: (1) Therapists assume that self-actualization and resolution of problems for women come from marriage and family, and they do not encourage gratification from work and careers. In other words, therapists encourage traditional sex roles. (2) Therapists demonstrate lack of respect for women through demeaning comments and labels. (3) Therapists use sexist psychoanalytic concepts, such as penis envy and vaginal orgasm. (4) Therapists have a double standard for male and female sexual activities. They respond to women as sex objects and sometimes have sexual relationships with female clients.

The conclusions drawn from the report reinforce the assumption that not only is sex-role stereotyping widespread in our society in general, but it is also believed to be widespread within the mental-health professions. These sex biases affect the quality of professional services available, especially for female clients. It is an interesting sign of the times that no task force has yet been created to examine the effects of sex biases on men.

Testing Personal Values and Biases

Whether you are a male or female therapist, counselor, educator, graduate student, or other person interested in mental-health issues, it is likely that you carry sex-role values and biases from your own upbringing which are reinforced by contacts with our daily culture. Also, your professional training has almost certainly been affected by the beliefs and biases held by your teachers, professors, and supervisors. To what degree do stereotypes operate within you to affect your perceptions of your male and female clients and the goals and treatment you plan for them? Do you treat female clients differently than male clients? Are you more comfortable (or uncomfortable) with female clients than with male clients? Male or female, the socialization process in each of us usually affects our perceptions of others. If we do not understand or recognize our own biases or prejudices, it is possible to maim a client psychologically.

One of the most powerful and effective ways to recognize signs of having different values for female and male clients with similar life goals is to evaluate case studies of women and men in similar situations. Sex-biased views which may be obscured are sometimes revealed by this technique.

Case Study No. 1

Carla S is a twenty-eight-year-old married woman with two children, a boy four years old and a baby girl one year old. She is moderately attractive and dresses casually but neatly. She has a college degree with a double major in education and psychology. Following graduation from college, she worked as a seventh-grade teacher for three years, leaving her job when she was seven months pregnant with her first child. Her husband is an attorney and earns approximately $30,000 each year.

Carla voluntarily contacted the clinic/agency and referred herself as a client. She takes little or no medication, and this is her first experience with counseling.

During the first few counseling sessions, Carla described herself as anxious and depressed. She appeared fairly calm on the surface, but smiled nervously and did not seem entirely at ease. She described her children as "happy and healthy," and stated that although she loves them and enjoys them she also feels "trapped" by them and has no time for herself. She seems to get along fairly well with her husband, but she stated she feels they are growing apart. Also she is not satisfied sexually and feels she would like this situation to improve. She stated that sexual contact with her husband is usually "pleasant" but "infrequent," about once every two weeks, and that often the children get in the way or she feels "too tired" or "not in the mood."

Carla stated that she feels she is "wasting her time" at home and that she would like to go back to work or, better yet, go to graduate school in psychology. Her undergraduate grades were excellent and she has completed the Graduate Record Exams and scored very well. To return to school, however, would mean that she and her family would have to move, since the university is over four hours away. Her husband is not in favor of her returning to school and feels that since they don't need the income from her employment, she should remain at home, care for the children, and possibly find some part-time volunteer work.

At this point, you as a mental-health professional should think about your tentative reactions to Carla and her situation. Consider all aspects of her case, including her views of it, your views of it, and how your views differ from hers. Try to identify what assumptions and expectations you have made about Carla based on your views of sex roles.

Case Study No. 2

Carl S is a twenty-eight-year-old married man with two children, a boy four years old and a baby girl one year old. He is moderately attractive and dresses casually but neatly. He has a college degree with a double major in education and psychology. Since graduation, he has worked as a seventh-grade teacher. His wife is an attorney and earns approximately $30,000 per year.

Carl voluntarily contacted the clinic/agency and referred himself as a client. He takes little or no medication, and this is his first experience with counseling.

During the first few counseling sessions, Carl described himself as anxious and depressed. He appeared fairly calm on the surface, but smiled nervously and did not seem entirely at ease. He described his children as "happy and healthy," and stated that although he loves them and enjoys them he sometimes feels "trapped" by them and has no time for himself. He seems to get along fairly well with his wife, but stated he feels they are growing apart. Also he is not satisfied sexually and would like this situation to improve. He stated that sexual contact with his wife is "pleasant" but "infrequent," about once every two weeks, and that often the children get in the way or he feels "too tired" or "not in the mood."

Carl stated he feels he is "wasting his time" at work, and he would like to quit work and stay home with the children or, better yet, go to graduate school in psychology. His undergraduate grades were excellent and he has taken the Graduate Record Exams and scored very highly. To return to school, however, would mean that he and his family would have to move, since the university is over four hours away. His wife is not in favor of his returning to school and feels that since they can afford a full-time babysitter he should remain with his teaching job and possibly find some additional hobbies or sports interests.

Again, at this point, what are your tentative reactions to Carl and his situation? Consider how your views of his situation differ from his views, and try to identify what kinds of assumptions and expectations you have made about Carl based on your views of sex roles.

Think about your possible goals and methods of interaction with Carla and Carl and whether they are different or similar. Consider possible differences in how you viewed the wife's/husband's views, the limited sexual satisfaction, the opportunities for graduate school, the possibility of having to move, the issue of working or not working, the consequences for the children, and the seriousness of the symptoms of anxiety and depression. Think about possible assumptions you have made about Carla's/Carl's ethnic background or race.

You will probably find that you have had some different expectations and would have chosen some different directions for working with Carla or Carl. It seems reasonable to expect different perceptions in a society such as ours which encourages sex-role stereotypes. You may now be more aware of how your own biases can affect how you work with your clients and how sex biases within a society can limit the potential of both women and men. "Value-free psychotherapy is a myth" (Bart, 1971), and it is sometimes painful to realize that men and women trained as mental-health professionals operate with sex biases, even when we are verbally aware of the issues.

We have now looked at sex roles and stereotypes in action within the general society and also within the mental-health professions and within ourselves. It seems appropriate that we now turn to a discussion of the development of sex roles and stereotypes to enhance our understanding of how these separate standards of behavior for men and women begin and are reinforced during infancy and childhood.

Development of Sex Roles and Stereotypes

Sex roles and stereotypes begin to influence people's lives even before they are born and, in fact, may sometimes determine whether or not conception and pregnancy are desired. Investigators have found that the likelihood of having a third child is greater in families if the first two children are both girls than if they are both boys. Also the interval between the birth of the first child and conception of the second is longer when the first child is a boy (Pohlman, 1969). When asked whether or not they had a preference for the sex of their first-born child, two-thirds of the young adults questioned expressed a preference and, of these, 92 percent wanted a boy. When asked about the sex of an only child, two-thirds of the women and over 80 percent of the men wanted this only child to be male (Peterson and Peterson, 1973). In a similar study, over 1500 married women under forty years of age, representing forty-eight states, and one-fourth of their husbands were interviewed, and the preference was clearly for boys. Almost twice as many people indicated that they preferred boys than preferred girls, and the pattern was more pronounced among the men (Hoffman, 1977).

Studies of pregnant women have indicated that mothers of daughters are happier about a new pregnancy than mothers who have sons. Furthermore, during the last three months of pregnancy, mothers tend to respond to the activity of the unborn child in a sex-differentiated manner. Typically, when the fetus is active and moves a great deal, the mother interprets this as an indication that the fetus is probably male (Lewis, 1972).

The strong preference for a male child, which has been found in many studies, provides a demonstration of the influence of sex roles and stereotypes. Apparently the underlying assumption is that males are somehow more valuable human beings than females.

The influences of sex roles and stereotypes become more apparent when the babies are born. It appears that parents label and view their newborn child differently as a function of the infant's sex. Parents tend to have different expectations for sons and daughters from birth even though information about the infants is minimal. Fathers typically refer to their newborn children with greater stereotypical expectations than mothers. They expect their sons to be aggressive and athletic and their daughters to be sweet, pretty, fragile, and delicate, and they describe their newborn in these terms. Fathers of infant daughters spend more time talking to their daughters than to their sons in infancy and exhibit more apprehensive concern over their infant daughter's well-being (Rebelsky and Hanks, 1971; Pedersen and Robson, 1969).

In a related study (Rubin, Provenzano, and Luria, 1974), psychologists interviewed the parents of newborn infants within twenty-four hours after the infant's birth. There were no objective differences between the babies in birth weight, length, or any other physical or neurological characteristics. There were no reports of medical problems during any of the pregnancies or deliveries and all infants in the sample were full-term at the time of birth. Thirty pairs of first-time parents were interviewed. As found in previous studies, fathers were especially influenced by the sex of the infants. Fathers described their daughters as more inattentive, delicate, and weak than the mothers did, and fathers rated their sons as stronger, better coordinated, and more alert than the mothers rated them. Parents of the girls described their infants as little, beautiful, pretty, and cute more often than parents of boys, while parents of boys described their infants as big more often than did parents of girls. Only one result was unexpected. Mothers rated sons as more cuddly than daughters, while fathers rated daughters as cuddlier than sons. The investigators labeled this finding the "oedipal" effect.

As an example of how this early stereotyping can affect boys and girls, Sandra and Daryl Bem (1976) have devised a "predictability test." According to the Bems, when a boy is born, if you ask people to predict what he will be doing twenty-five years later, they will say that it is difficult or impossible to predict because the boy has so many options and opportunities for development, especially if he is white and middle class. But if the newborn child is a girl, people will usually predict with some confidence how she will be spending her time twenty-five years later. Her individuality doesn't have to be considered. She is expected to become a wife and a mother, and all other ambitions are expected to be secondary. Males are also discouraged from developing certain desirable traits such as sensitivity and nurturance, but even without these traits they have a much wider range of opportunities available to them than do women in our society.

Sex Differences in Infancy and Childhood

The physical differences distinguishing females from males have encouraged psychologists, sociologists, and other investigators to search for additional biological, psychological, and sociocultural differences. Even though women and men are not opposities of each other and are probably much more alike than different, the emphasis has been on investigating and categorizing the hypothesized differences between them.

Investigators have felt that if they could document evidence on infants, supposedly before society has had an impact on the babies, the results and conclusions would stem directly from biological influence. Many hypothesized that sex-role differences in adults would be affected by the sex differences observed in infants and children. Investigators have also been interested in the effects of socialization on infants and children and have hypothesized that the different treatment accorded to male and female babies by parents, schools, and others would explain the learning of the different sex roles that continues into their adult life. Unfortunately, many of the studies that document infant and childhood sex differences are contradictory or complicated by flaws. Many other studies that have not demonstrated sex differences have been ignored or rejected.

An intensive review and integration of the extensive research literature on sex differences was conducted by Maccoby and Jacklin (1974). Most of the studies included were comparisons of male and female behavior in infancy and childhood. On the basis of their review, these investigators concluded that the results from many of the studies depend upon the particular sample of boys and girls studied and on the specific situations in which they are observed. Furthermore, they concluded that boys and girls are apparently more similar to one another than they are different and that they share many fundamental needs and abilities. Even during childhood, when socialization pressures to learn appropriate sex roles are extremely intense, boys and girls exhibit similar behavior, though they are probably accumulating information about the different sex roles they are expected to acquire.

Maccoby and Jacklin acknowledge that there are some sex differences in infancy and childhood that are fairly well established by existing research. Girls are developmentally ahead of boys at birth, and this advantage continues throughout childhood. At birth, central nervous system maturation is advanced for females, and by school age, girls are estimated to be at least six months ahead of boys in development. This advanced development probably accounts for the fact that during infancy and childhood girls have greater verbal ability than boys. It is also well established that males are more aggressive than females, beginning as early as age two when social play begins. Although aggression declines for both sexes with age, males remain more aggressive throughout college. From early ages, other males are the primary targets of male aggression with females less often chosen as victims. The greater aggression in males apparently has a biological component, since levels of aggression have been demonstrated to be responsive to sex hormones. Even though most aggressive behavior for both sexes appears to be learned, males are more biologically predisposed for learning in this area. However, these findings do not indicate that girls are submissive. Investigators have found that girls are socialized to use more subtle forms of aggression than boys, such as verbal assaults or interpersonal rejection, but that they are no more likely to withdraw under attack than boys (Feshbach and Feshbach, 1973).

Parent Behavior and Sex-Role Socialization

There is some evidence that there are differences in parental treatment of boys and girls during infancy, and some maintain that these differences in treatment could account for the differences in verbal ability and aggressiveness in boys and girls. Investigators Goldberg and Lewis (1969) observed that mothers of female infants touched their babies more often than did mothers of male infants. They also talked to and played with their daughters more often. By thirteen months, the girls talked to and touched their mothers more often than the boys did. In another study, Moss (1967) observed that at three weeks male infants are held more and stimulated more by their mothers, but by three months the mothers of girls are touching and handling their infants more often. Moss observed other differences in treatment for male and female infants and concluded that from birth on the babies are being given reinforcement for appropriate behavior. He tentatively suggested that verbal ability in girls and aggressiveness in boys were being selectively encouraged in the infants he observed. Most of the studies on infants, however, have indicated that there are few sex differences in the behavior of infants and that parents tend to treat infants of both sexes the same more than differently.

During childhood, researchers have found that parents have different sex-role expectations for their sons and daughters. In a recent study, the differences in bedroom furnishings for boys and girls were examined as indications of parental expectations for their children. The rooms of girls contained more floral furnishings and more dolls. The rooms of boys contained more animal furnishings, more educational toys, more athletic equipment, more art materials, and more vehicles (Rheingold and Cook, 1975). This investigation revealed obvious differences in the treatment of boys and girls during childhood.

Other recent investigations have observed the behavior of adult men and women when responding to children. In one study, a three-year-old child was alternately labeled as a boy and as a girl. Adults observed the child's behavior as he/she performed various activities on videotape and then evaluated the child. Cross-sex effects were most significant. Men were more positive in their evaluations when they thought the child was a girl, and women rated the child more positively when they were told the child was a boy (Gurwitz and Dodge, 1975). In a similar investigation, adults observed videotapes of two seventeen-month-old children, each of whom was described sometimes as a boy and sometimes a girl. When the subjects were asked to describe and interpret the behavior of the children, the adult men were more likely to rate the children in a stereotyped manner by attributing independence, aggressiveness, alertness, and activity to the child labeled a boy and qualities such as passivity, delicacy, and dependency to the child labeled a girl. In this investigation, sex of adult and sex of the children interacted to indicate that the adult men placed greater emphasis on sex-role stereotypes than adult women (Meyer and Sobieszek, 1972). In yet another related study, a four-year-old child's voice was alternately presented as either that of a boy or girl to parents of nursery-school-age children. Fathers were more permissive in both aggressive and dependency situations with girls, while mothers were more permissive with boys (Rothbart and Maccoby, 1966).

These studies further support the hypothesis that children are subjected to differential treatment by parents and other adults on the basis of the sexes of the adults and of the children and that adult sex-role expectations differ for boys and girls. Apparently, it is the father who is especially likely to treat the children of the two sexes differently, and extremes of affection or authority from the father may have marked effects on his children. Some investigators have concluded that authoritarian fathers exhibiting high degrees of nurturance and protectiveness when interacting with their daughters can influence the development of dependency and oversocialization in their daughters instead of the qualities of independence, initiative, and self-sufficiency that they instill into the behavior of their sons (Bronfenbrenner, 1961).

Despite all of the apparent pressures for sex-role differences in childhood, Maccoby and Jacklin (1974) have found that the behavior of boys and girls is more similar than divergent during this stage of development as well as during the infancy stage. Even the long-accepted hypotheses that boys are punished more severely than girls for dependency and passivity and that girls are punished more severely than boys for aggressiveness were not supported by the review of the literature. In fact, it appears that boys may actually be punished more harshly for aggressive behavior than girls and that parents do not generally approve or accept aggression in either sex. There is some evidence that socialization pressures may be more intense for boys than for girls and that boys receive more physical punishment as well as more rewards, especially for specifically sex-type behaviors.

Implications for Mental-Health Professionals

Many people who utilize the mental-health services of a clinic, an agency, or a private practitioner are experiencing problems related to sex-role requirements and expectations for children. Adults who are concerned about their role as parents, "problem" children who are referred by their parents or the school system, and parents and children treated as family groups are often having difficulty understanding and dealing with the different socialization pressures for young girls and boys.

The clinician who is aware of sex-role issues and understands the stereotypes and sex-role biases that can develop during infancy and childhood can often help alleviate fears and problems. Sometimes, providing specific information can be helpful. For example, parents who are concerned because their young son does not seem to be developing as rapidly physically or intellectually as his older sister did at the same age may be relieved to learn (after physical problems have been ruled out) that girls are typically more advanced than boys in development during infancy and childhood, especially in verbal ability. Or, in another case, parents may be relieved to know that although boys may be more likely to demonstrate overt aggression after age two, many young girls are also aggressive and this behavior alone does not mean that there is something wrong with the child or that the parents are inadequate.

Since the behavior of young boys and girls is typically more similar than different during infancy and childhood and since there are only a few biologically determined sex differences in behavior, the clinician should be aware that "problem behavior" during these early years is more likely to be caused by the expectations of the parents than by the characteristics of the particular child. Parents exert pressure upon their children to act "correctly," and often their own sex-role biases and fears are projected upon their children. As we noted earlier in this chapter, the relatively few studies that are available that include fathers as subjects have indicated that it is the father who typically holds the most stereotyped views and who may have the strongest influence upon sex-role development in his children. Therefore, it may be the fathers who especially need to get in touch with their own sex-role expectations for their children and to become aware of the responsibility they share for influencing the values and beliefs of their children.

Parents can learn that there are no harmful effects from letting children of both sexes play with similar kinds of toys and that their children may benefit from exposure and experience with both trucks and dolls or athletic equipment and art materials. Also, boys may be relieved to learn that it is sometimes permissible to cry or show emotions, and girls may be happier if they are sometimes encouraged to be independent and assertive.

Case Study Example

In a related case study, a thirty-year-old married woman with two children, ages three and six, referred herself for treatment because of symptoms of depression and feelings of inadequacy as a wife and mother. During the first therapy sessions she described herself as a failure in everything she tried and spoke frequently about hating herself. When asked about her family, she stated that her husband was a successful professional man and that her children were physically healthy but had "behavior problems." When asked for more information, she reluctantly and apologetically stated that both children were "just girls." She stated that she and her husband had wanted boys both times she had been pregnant and were bitterly disappointed when each girl was born. As therapy progressed, it became increasingly clear that both the client and her husband not only endorsed the strong, widespread preference of Americans for male children, but that they also believed intensely in the "positive" stereotyped roles for men and in the "negative," devalued stereotyped roles for women. The client had spent her whole life hating herself and other women, a biased view she had learned from her own parents and significant others in her life, and had married a man who loved her, but who also accepted the "fact" that she was "inferior" as a person. As parents, they were both teaching their daughters to regard themselves as inferior to boys, and the girls were responding by becoming "problems." Her depression and self-hatred had increased after her second daughter was born, since she had counted desperately on having a son to prove she could "do something right."

In this particular case, since the husband refused to participate in therapy, the client was seen individually and also in a group with other women where the focus of the group was on examining alternatives to stereotyped sex roles and on assertiveness training. After several months, her depression disappeared and her views of herself and her daughters began to change. As she changed, she began treating her daughters differently and their behavior began to "improve." However, her marriage deteriorated, and she and the children eventually left her husband to "get away from his destructive influence."

As a mental-health professional, consider this case and the results of the therapy. Think about how you would have reacted to this client and how you might have handled this case differently. Try to be aware of your own sex biases and your own feelings or lack of feelings of identification with the client, her husband, and/or her children.

In the next chapter, we will look at sources of sex-role socialization outside of the family.

2

Sex-Role Socialization Outside of the Family

Sex-Role Differences in Adolescence

During infancy and childhood, through the socialization process, girls and boys begin to acquire different information about appropriate future sex roles. It is not until adolescence, however, that major differences in sex-role behavior appear, and these differences are maintained throughout adult life. The advantage that girls had over boys in childhood because of their advanced development disappears during adolescence, and boys begin to excel in many areas. Socialization pressures increase during adolescence, and society reinforces different behavior for girls and boys. Boys are expected and encouraged to increase their efforts toward achievement and career goals and to develop their intellectual and physical abilities to their fullest extent. Girls, on the other hand, often find themselves in a "double-bind" (Horner, 1972) conflict between achievement and their prescribed sex role. Achievement is no longer highly rewarded for a girl and is often seen as incompatible with more highly regarded traits such as popularity and sociability. Girls are often not encouraged to develop their full intellectual or physical potential; rather, they are encouraged to maintain a flexible identity that will be compatible with future roles as wife and mother.

During adolescence boys become superior to girls in visual-spatial tasks and in mathematical ability, and these differences increase into adulthood, while girls' performances in school and on ability tests begin to decrease (Maccoby and Jacklin, 1974). Although parents continue to have a great deal of influence on the development of sex roles for boys and girls during adolescence, the major influences during these years are the school environment and the peer group.

The School Environment

The influence of the school environment on the development and socialization of sex roles can be considerable. One of the first messages communicated to girls and boys at school is that girls are less important than boys. The educational system has traditionally reinforced existing sex-role stereotypes and has exerted pressure on boys and girls to conform to appropriate roles. Teachers and guidance counselors have tended to reinforce conformity and encourage boys and girls to pursue different goals and engage in separate activities. Girls have often been discouraged from taking advanced courses such as physics or calculus and, until recently, were completely excluded from the more strenuous and prestigious sports activities and athletic competition. Boys, on the other hand, have been expected to participate in sports and to take science and math courses but to avoid "feminine" courses such as languages, home economics, or typing.

Teachers can directly influence sex roles by conveying feelings about appropriate or inappropriate behavior. They can reinforce students for specific behavior and can ignore or ridicule behavior they feel is inappropriate. Textbooks and lectures only rarely contain information about women, and when women are mentioned, they are almost always presented according to the stereotyped view. Teachers and textbooks have traditionally adopted the male character as the model or standard for learning and achievement and have minimized or ignored the contributions made by women.

Although sex-role pressures exerted by the school environment intensify during adolescence, the influence of the schools begins much earlier. One recent study of teachers and children in nursery school classrooms provides research evidence that teachers do treat boys and girls differently. Even though the teachers in the study were not aware that they were treating the sexes differently, the investigators observed that the teachers reinforced boys for being aggressive by responding immediately to boys who misbehaved and giving them a great deal of attention. All of the teachers paid more attention to the boys and gave the boys twice as much individual instruction on a task as they gave girls. Boys were rewarded more for academic achievement, and girls were reinforced for being dependent and staying close to the teachers. Boys were encouraged to be creative and independent in their activities, while teachers were much more likely to take over and complete a task for a girl (Serbin and O'Leary, 1975). Even though the sex-role messages from the teachers were often subtle and covert, the children were observed to be aware of them and to be responding in sex-differentiated ways. Several other studies have demonstrated that these early influences from the school environment continue throughout a student's academic career and have considerable effect on a student's sex-role identity as well as academic ambitions (Cherry, 1975; Douvan and Adelson, 1966).

Students are also exposed to other subtle sex-role-related messages. Most elementary school teachers are women, but most principals and administrators are men. As the age of the student and complexity of the material increase, so do the prestige and salary of the teachers. Female teachers are most prevalent in the early years when material is simple and prestige is low, and male teachers predominate in the junior high and high school years when the work is more difficult and the prestige is higher (Mickish, 1971).

The Peer Group

Probably the most influential enforcers of sex roles during adolescence are the members of the peer group. These groups typically encourage activities which are greatly influenced by sex-role stereotypes. Acceptance by the peer group entails conforming and subscribing to the values and goals of the group, and deviance is punished by the threat of withdrawal of support and friendship. The impact of the peer group becomes obvious during adolescence, especially to parents and other adults, even though the adolescents themselves may not be consciously aware of the extent of the influence of the group on their behavior.

The pressures for conformity to peer values can be intense for both boys and girls. Many adolescent girls believe that development of their intellectual abilities will have only negative results and should not be pursued since they will always be less important and less capable than most men (Freeman, 1971). Boys, on the other hand, are pressured to attain athletic and sexual success and high academic achievement.

The influence of peer groups decreases after adolescence but continues throughout adulthood. For the college-oriented girl, socialization pressure from her peers and environment continues throughout college and is probably most intense during her last two years as an undergraduate rather than in high school. During her junior and senior years in college, pressures for more traditional feminine sex-role activities that were postponed from early adolescence become especially severe, and she will have to deal with these role conflicts at this later stage in her life. Also in high school and even more so in college, students elected to leadership positions such as class or student-body president tend to be male. The powerful positions that are held by women are more often appointive rather than elective (Frazier and Sadker, 1973).

Until adolescence, girls in our society have greater freedom to engage in a wider range of behavior than boys. Especially in the middle class, girls are allowed to engage in such activities as wearing boys' clothes or climbing trees or playing ball without fear of punishment or censure, whereas boys are expected to conform to social norms much earlier and will often be disciplined severely for wearing girls' clothes or skipping rope or playing with dolls. Boys show stable, same-sex preferences at an early age, because the consequences of deviating from the norm are painful and harsh. Once they have identified with the male role, however, they are rewarded by being given the privileges and status that accompany their sex role. Girls, on the other hand, are pushed gently and more subtly into a sex role that is neither rewarded nor preferred by society. They are encouraged to perform behaviors that are held in low esteem and for which they receive little recognition or satisfaction.

Sex-Role Differences during Adulthood

The effects of the socialization process during infancy, childhood, and adolescence are very apparent by adulthood. When adults in our society are requested to identify themselves, women and men define themselves quite differently and usually in accordance with established sex-role requirements. Men identify themselves in terms of their occupations, schools they have attended, clubs or organizations they belong to, and, in general, goals and achievements throughout their lives. Sometimes they also indicate their marital status and whether or not they have children. Women, on the other hand, tend to identify themselves in terms of other people and most often in terms of the wife and mother roles. They define themselves as someone's wife and someone's mother. A woman is Mrs. John Doe and Bobby and Susie Doe's mother. Even if she is employed and/or has a college degree or two, she usually does not identify herself in these terms. The methods of socializing women and the content of the feminine sex role apparently encourage overidentification with others and discourage the development of a sense of self as a separate person. Since there are different cultural expectations for men and women and since they are raised differently, differences in sex-role identities are not surprising. Although the female role does have positive components, such as nurturance and warmth, these are not the traits that receive the highest reinforcement in our society, and women and men tend to perceive that most of the valuable traits belong to men. In the absence of independent achievement, women measure their worth from the response of other people and evaluate their roles as inferior. Our society rewards masculine endeavors with money, power, and status, but few prestigious rewards are given for the roles of housewife and mother. Consequently, it is not surprising that more adult women (20–31 percent) than adult men (4 percent) report recalling conscious desires to belong to the other sex (Sherman, 1971).

Having examined some of the ways that people outside of the family, including teachers, guidance counselors, and peers, influence sex-role socialization, it seems appropriate to consider how we, as mental-health professionals, might be able to help minimize or alleviate sex-role biases and problems that surface during adolescent years.

Implications for Mental-Health Professionals

Although the results of sex-role bias in the educational system usually don't become obvious until adolescence, the socialization pressures begin as soon as children enter school. Therefore, changes in the educational process need to be made at all grade levels.

Teachers need to become aware of their own sex-role values and biases so that they can understand how they subtly—and often not so subtly—encourage and reinforce separate behavior patterns for boys and girls. Education majors in college should be required to take courses on sex roles and could be helped to get in touch with their own feelings about sex roles and stereotypes through group discussions and role-play sessions. One of the most powerful tools for emphasizing the impact of biased behavior is the videotape. Both student teachers and veteran teachers are often amazed and sometimes horrified to watch a videotape of their behavior in the classroom. Even teachers who have insisted that they treat all of their students equally have had to reassess their own values and motives after seeing themselves in action.

Counselors and school psychologists can also benefit from training that stresses an awareness of sex-role stereotypes and biases. Mental-health professionals in the schools not only need to become aware of their own feelings about sex roles, but also need to become aware of the sex biases that are built into many of the test materials they have traditionally used to measure abilities, achievement, vocational interests, and personality adjustment. We will be discussing test biases and some of the new testing materials that are being developed to remedy these biases in another chapter. However, the widespread use of sex-biased tests in the school system should be at least mentioned here as an example of what needs to be changed to stop sex-role stereotyping in the educational process.

Men and Women as Role Models in Education

The majority of teachers in the elementary schools are women, and the majority of college teachers and professors are men. It is easy to conclude that one of the reasons many boys have trouble adjusting to school is the overly "feminized" atmosphere during the elementary school years. Similarly, it might be concluded that one of the reasons girls often stop achieving during high school and college is that they no longer have same-sex role models to encourage their achievement. The "obvious" solution, then, would be to provide *incentives* for more men to teach or become counselors in the elementary grades and provide *opportunities* for more women to teach high-level courses in high schools and universities. While this might alleviate part of the problem, at least in terms of the visibility of role models of both sexes, unless the teachers and counselors are aware of sex-role issues and influences, they could actually encourage *more* stereotyping rather than less. This might be true especially in the lower grade levels, since some men have been found to demand more stereotyped behavior from children than women do.

A more complete solution might be one where teachers and counselors are taught to be in touch with their own feelings and positive characteristics and are also taught how to convey these characteristics to both boys and girls. If boys and girls are exposed to the positive characteristics of both sexes throughout the educational process and are allowed and encouraged to develop all of these characteristics, they may grow up to be adults who are no longer forced so completely into one inflexible role or the other.

Textbooks

Textbook contents must also be changed to eliminate sex-role stereotypes. If children believe portrayals in textbooks, they believe that: (1) The majority of the people in the world are men and almost all of the *important* people are men. (2) Most animals and fantasy characters are male. (3) There are at least six times as many occupations for men as for women. The opportunities for men include exciting jobs like fireman, doctor, astronaut, and policeman. Women don't work if they are mothers, and if they aren't mothers they can be teachers, nurses, secretaries, circus fat ladies, or witches. (4) Girls hold dolls, sew, jump rope, cook, cry, and look bewildered, while boys swim, sail, climb mountains, play ball, and build things (Women on Words and Images, 1972).

Many high school and college texts speak of "mankind" as if humans were only men. History textbooks concentrate on the study of our "forefathers," and even if the words were changed to "the people who built our nation," it does not change the fact that the majority of the people discussed in the history texts are male. In math and science textbooks, males portrayed as examples use scientific equipment, experiment, and achieve, while females continue the cooking and sewing they began in the elementary textbooks. One textbook actually defines "standard English" as the language spoken by the "educated professional" and "his wife," as if all educated professionals were men (Burr, Dunn, and Farquhar, 1972).

We will discuss language usage and other forms of communication in more detail later in this chapter. Textbooks, however, provide some of the most striking examples of how sex biases are communicated.

Changing stereotyped stories and examples in textbooks may not always be welcomed by students or their parents, however. For example, Jennings (1975) found that children preferred a story in which a girl wanted to be a ballerina and a boy wanted to be a mail carrier to one in which the girl wanted to be a mail carrier and the boy a ballerina. Nevertheless, the children did recall the context of the reversed sex-role story more accurately. Children do notice the sex roles portrayed in stories and, even if nothing else, remember the ones that are counter to expectations.

Counseling and Therapy with Adolescents and Their Parents

Adolescence can be a difficult time for both adolescents and their parents. Socialization pressures may become intense and sometimes unbearable, and it is not unusual for troubled adolescents to seek help themselves or to be referred to mental-health professionals for help.

The clinician who is aware of sex-role issues will be able to understand the intense pressure on boys to achieve academically as well as athletically and the anxiety that can result from this pressure. On the other hand, adolescent girls may be anxious and depressed as their reinforcement for achievement disappears and they are forced into competition with other girls for the attention of boys and men. The clinician who understands these pressures may be able to help minimize or alleviate some of the resulting symptoms and "problem behavior" by helping adolescents to become aware of alternatives to stereotyped roles and expectations and encouraging them to concentrate on what is best for them as individuals. In addition, anxious parents can often be helped to understand the influence of the peer group and friends during adolescence and can learn to cope with the trauma of the adolescent struggle for autonomy.

Case Study Example

In a related case study, John A, a sixteen-year-old boy, is referred to therapy by his parents. He is a high school senior and has maintained an A average in a difficult college-preparatory curriculum. He has completed the high school requirements in three years instead of the usual four and is due to graduate in a few weeks. John has agreed to a consultation visit, and his parents are anxious to schedule an appointment.

Both John and his parents attend the first consultation session. All three appear very tense and there appears to be an undercurrent of anger, especially between John and his father. John is dressed casually in jeans and a denim shirt, and his parents are more formally attired, his father in a suit and his mother in an attractive dress. Mr. A owns and operates an insurance agency and Mrs. A works part-time as a bookkeeper in the agency and also cares for their two other children, both girls, ages twelve and nine. Both parents are college graduates and have high expectations for all three of their children, but especially for John.

During the session, Mr. A does most of the talking. He states that John had always been an intelligent, well-adjusted, athletic, and energetic boy until about a year ago when he began to "change." According to Mr. A, during the past year John has been spending more and more time with his "undesirable" friends from school, has lost interest in sports, and has been refusing to participate with the rest of the family in planning vacation trips or in sharing household duties or even in showing up on time for dinner. Mr. A further states that when John is home he spends most of his time in his room either reading or listening to records and that he is rude and surly to his mother and sisters. The final straw, according to Mr. A, came a few weeks ago when John announced that he had decided he was not going to college and that he intends to leave home when he graduates to travel with friends and to find work wherever he can to support himself. Mr. A stated that both he and his wife feel that John is becoming seriously maladjusted and that they are not knowledgeable enough to deal with the problem themselves. Mrs. A has been nodding in agreement with her husband's statements.

As Mr. A is speaking, John is looking out of the window and appears to be trying to look indifferent to what is being said. When he is asked how he feels about the situation, however, he looks angry and states that his parents don't really understand his situation and haven't really given him a chance to explain why he doesn't want to go to college. At this point, both Mr. A and Mrs. A interrupt John to protest about his last statement, and Mr. A and

John begin shouting at each other. John stops shouting and begins looking out the window again, which makes Mr. A even more angry, and Mrs. A begins to cry.

You are a mental-health professional and are aware of the sex-role socialization pressures that affect most adolescents. You are also aware of the ways in which sex roles have shaped the values and expectations of many adults in our society. In light of what you know about sex-role issues, and taking your own views and possible sex-role biases into account, think about how you might decide to proceed with John and his parents. What kinds of goals might you establish? What type of therapy, if any, might you recommend? What types of therapy techniques or testing materials would you use or not use in this case? Think about how you feel toward John, Mr. A, and Mrs. A. If you identify with one of them more than the others, try to be aware of this in yourself and relate it to your own views and values.

Additional Sources of Sex-Role Socialization

Family, the educational system, and friends all have lasting influences on sex-role socialization. There are also several other sources of influence in our society that exert pressure upon boys and girls and men and women to behave in sex-differentiated ways. These additional sources of sex-role socialization include our use of communication and language, as well as the influences of the various media in our society, including television and movies.

Language

By looking at the way we customarily talk and express ourselves verbally, we can gain insight into the way we feel about ourselves and others. According to Weitz (1977), language, in regard to sex roles, can be separated into two parts. The first part concerns the structure of the language itself and the way in which language often is divided into so-called "women's" and "men's" languages (Bodine, 1975). The second part concerns the different ways women and men use language to express themselves. Examples of the differences in language structure include the pronouns "him" or "her" in the English language as well as "*elles*" and "*ils*" meaning "they," as women, and "they," as men, in French. Another aspect of the form of the language is the "marking" of certain words (Weitz, 1977). In English, unmarked words are considered to be masculine; for example, "doctor," "professor," or "writer." When the person is a woman, an identifying suffix must be added to indicate or "mark" the fact; for example, "woman doctor," "female professor," "lady writer." Probably the most obvious example of this tendency to identify with the male standard is the use of the word "he" to denote any person of unknown gender.

The second aspect of language is the different usage of language by men and women. One of the most thorough investigations of the uses of language has been reported by a "woman linguist," Robin Lakoff, in her book *Language and a Woman's Place* (1975). Lakoff maintains that men and women are taught to use language differently and that language treats men and women differently. For example, girls are usually criticized or made fun of for expressing themselves forcefully or using "rough talk" because talking aggressively is an accepted part of boys' language but not of girls' or women's language. On the other hand, girls are allowed to name colors precisely, like "beige," "lavender," or "mauve," because this is part of "women's" language, but boys would usually be ostracized for describing colors in such detail. As Lakoff points out, it is interesting to note that men's language is being increasingly adopted by women, but women's language is not being adopted by men.

Women are much more likely than men to use "tag questions" when making a statement in order to avoid committing themselves or accepting responsibility for the statement. For example, "It's really hot in here, isn't it?" or "He was just here, wasn't he?" These questions at the end of a sentence give the impression that the speakers are unsure of themselves and are seeking confirmation even though they may know precisely what they are talking about. Lakoff maintains that women prejudice the case against themselves by their use of language. Perhaps that is one of the reasons she chose to illustrate the cover of her book with a picture of a woman with a band-aid over her mouth.

Our language also treats women differently than men. In English, women are often referred to as "ladies," a term that is condescending and implies a frivolous nature, according to Lakoff, or as "girls," a term that implies immaturity and irresponsibility. Men are seldom called "boys" past the age of adolescence, but women of all ages are referred to as girls. Words like "mistress" and "spinster" also have negative connotations, even though their counterparts for men, "master" and "bachelor," are at least neutral terms. In other examples, since men are usually defined by what they do in the world and women are usually defined in terms of their sexuality and the men in their lives, the statement "He's a professional" may be interpreted quite differently from the statement "She's a professional." Also, when a traditional marriage service concludes, the couple becomes "man" and "wife." The man is a man before and after marriage, but the woman becomes a wife, a change that is further symbolized by her adopting the man's last name.

When men and women converse as couples, Zimmerman and West (1975) found that men tend to interrupt their partners more than women and use the interruptions to control the topics of the conversation. Women are silent more than men, and conversation topics introduced by women tend to be dropped in favor of those introduced by men (Fishman, 1965). In other words, men are more successful than women in controlling mixed-sex conversations, in spite of the stereotypes of the talkative woman and the man who can't get a word in edgewise.

Not all communication is verbal. We have discussed some of the ways that language contributes to sex-role socialization, and we are now ready to look at the influences of nonverbal forms of communication, such as touch, eye contact, personal space, and gestures.

Nonverbal Communication

Touching is a nonverbal way to express every emotion from love to anger. Men and women not only use touch differently, they also respond differently to being touched. According to Henley (1973), women are more likely to be touched. Women also respond more positively to being touched, and Henley maintains this is due at least in part to status differences between men and women. Between persons of different status positions, the dominant one will do more of the touching and the subordinate one will be touched more often. For example, an employer is more likely to touch an employee than vice versa, and a doctor is more likely to touch a patient or a teacher a student. Therefore, the fact that men touch women more than women touch men is not surprising, since the message is that the initiator has some power over the person being touched. Women may also have had more experience with being touched since same-sex touching is more allowable for girls and women than for men (Deaux, 1976). Except for formal handshakes, American men rarely touch other men.

Smiling is another way of communicating. Women smile more often than men even when the message of their smile is unclear or even negative (Deaux, 1976). Animals have been observed to "smile" as a gesture to indicate submissiveness when confronted by a superior, and some feminists have suggested that a woman's smile is a way of affirming her inferior status. However, smiles may also communicate happiness, nervousness, greeting, and encouragement, or they may be used to reduce tension or soften negative impact (Mehrabian, 1972). In a related study with parents and their children, Bugental et al. (1971) found that fathers tended to smile only when they were saying positive things, but mothers would smile even when they were saying negative things to their children. In judging the parents, the children tended to believe the verbal messages from their mothers and to ignore their smiles, but they believed their fathers' smiles indicated friendliness.

Women tend to spend more time looking directly at another person than men, and they also seem to rely more heavily on this form of nonverbal communication (Exline, 1965). At the same time, however, low self-esteem and feelings of inferiority are associated with the avoidance of direct eye contact, and again it is the woman who is most likely to avoid a direct glance or be the first to look away, unless she wants the interaction to continue (Libby and Yaklevich, 1973).

In terms of personal space or territory, studies suggest that women have less territory and take up less personal space than men. Also, this smaller space is more frequently violated than that of men (Frieze and Ramsey, 1976). For example, men are more likely to have a den or library or special room in a house than women, and men are more likely to have a "special chair," like Archie Bunker. Men more often have private office space in the work world, and both men and women stand closer to women than to men. When a male or female experimenter stood very close to a woman or a man on the street, men tended to move away from the male experimenters in response to this space violation (Dobbs, 1972).

The evidence we have discussed suggests that sex-role stereotypes function on nonverbal as well as verbal levels. Now let us turn our attention to the influence of the media.

Media Messages

Anyone who goes to the movies or watches television sees many obvious examples of sex-role stereotyping. According to a survey by Gerbner and Gross (1976), almost everyone in America watches television, and half of the twelve-year-old children in this country watch an average of six or more hours per day. The typical teenager today has spent more time in front of the TV than in school and will often remember more of what he or she has learned by watching at home. Television can transmit ideas and images to millions of people at the same time, and there is no mystery in its messages about how men and women should look and behave.

Children's TV Programs

Children's television programs are particularly important since preschool children typically spend more time watching TV than doing any other activity except sleeping. Sternglanz and Serbin (1974) analyzed ten of the most popular children's programs and found striking differences in the ways they treated male and female characters. Four of the programs didn't have any regular female characters. Even with the all-male programs excluded from consideration, male characters outnumbered female characters two to one. Male characters were portrayed as aggressive, constructive, and helpful, and they were more likely to be rewarded for their behavior. Female characters, on the other hand, were usually portrayed as passive and deferent, and sometimes they were punished if they were too aggressive or active. Female characters were effective only when they used "magic" of some sort to manipulate others without their awareness. Even in such supposedly liberated programs such as "Sesame Street," which was not included in the Sternglanz and Serbin study, few female characters appear in other than stereotyped roles (Weitz, 1977).

Prime-Time Television

Adult programming doesn't fare much better, and the same stereotypes and sex ratios prevail. Prime-time TV portrays approximately two male characters for every female character and three-fourths of all leading characters are men (Women on Words and Images, 1975). Most TV women don't have jobs, and with the exceptions of Mary Tyler Moore, Charlie's Angels, and Angie Dickinson, those who do work or are successful often have special or "magic" powers. For example, Wonder Woman and the Bionic Woman have helped make female characters more popular, but when they aren't saving the world, Wonder Woman works as a secretary and the Bionic Woman teaches elementary school. As Tavris and Offir (1977) have pointed out, in order to land a job as a TV heroine a woman must be beautiful and young. A man who plays a hero, however, can be bald (Kojak), fat (Cannon), or even paralyzed (Ironside). Men are more likely than women to be dominant, competent, and successful, and even Charlie's Angels take their orders from an authoritative man.

In soap operas and situation comedies the number of roles for women and men are approximately equal since situations and problems of life *do* include women as well as men. In comedy series, men are as likely as women to be ridiculed. Situation comedies typically ridicule everybody, and since the home is considered the woman's territory, perhaps the man at home is an easy target. In the soap operas, women are often portrayed in a more sympathetic light than in the situation comedies or in the adventure shows, and this is probably due to the fact that almost all viewers are women. Overall, however, there are many more admirable and competent men on television than there are women.

Television Commercials

Television commercials exaggerate the stereotyped message even more and contribute importantly to the maintenance of sex roles. Women appear as product users who take care of their homes and families, do the shopping, and try to remain forever young and beautiful. Men, on the other hand, work and play competitive sports and often speak with authority to bewildered women who can't tell the difference between various brands of toilet tissue, laundry detergents, or headache remedies. Women on Words and Images (1975) analyzed commercials and found that 96 percent of the authoritative voice-overs are male, even though most of the characters portrayed in commercials are women. Advertising aimed at men often promotes the image of sexual conquest and competition or aggression. Professional athletes promote hair tonics and shaving creams and lotions to make a man smell like a man, and beautiful women appear to be standard features of sports cars. The Silva-Thins man is famous for his sadistic treatment of beautiful women, and even buying certain brands of beers enhances the gusto in life or serves as a reward after a strenuous game of football or basketball. Advertising agencies know that stereotyped messages sell products.

Movies

Movies, whether they are seen in theaters or on television, also perpetuate American sex-role stereotypes. In the 1950s women were viewed as sexual but dumb. They were fictional women who had no sexual needs but were there to cater to the sexual needs of men (Haskell, 1973). Marilyn Monroe became the standard for this image of women. At the same time, coexisting with the Marilyn Monroe image was the domestic woman seeking love and marriage for fulfillment. Like the sex object, the image of this woman was developed and processed according to male preferences and standards. Doris Day has been cited as the perfect example of this pleasant, domestic characterization of women (Weitz, 1977).

In the late 1960s and the 1970s women became sexually active and independent, but they were also often punished for their escapades. Men have continued to dominate the film industry and to determine the images of the women presented (Mellon, 1973). Even in films during the late 1970s such as *The Goodbye Girl, Julia,* or *The Turning Point,* in which women played the leading roles, the heroines did not fare very well. In *The Goodbye Girl,* the heroine was left crying and clinging to a guitar with the hope that her lover would return someday; in *Julia,* the active, aggressive, politically oriented heroine lost a leg and was finally violently killed; and in *The Turning Point,* both heroines were left wondering whether they had made the right choices in their lives, but the one who chose domesticity still had her family, was not alone, and could presumably take vicarious pleasure in her daughter's success.

It is interesting that there is little separate critical treatment of male images in movies. However, it's obvious in most films that violence and power and aggression are the main themes. War movies, Westerns, and gangster films have always been popular. Besides aggression, men display cunning, intelligence, and sexual prowess. However, some of the closest and most affectionate relationships have been between men and other men rather than between men and women. For example, in *Women in Love* there was much more affection shared by Alan Bates and Oliver Reed, though not sexual, than either man shared with his wife; and more recently, Paul Newman and Robert Redford shared more affection for each other than for the women in *Butch Cassidy and the Sundance Kid* and *The Sting*. The message seems to be that men can love women, but they can love and *like* other men.

Influences of the Media

The problem of proving a connection between stereotyped media messages and behavior in real life is similar to one that researchers face when they try to show that people will imitate TV violence. In the laboratory, children will usually imitate violent behavior they see on film (Bandura et al., 1963), but it is harder to prove how viewers react outside of the laboratory. An ideal test would be to find groups of children who are similar in intelligence and home environments and expose half of them to television and movies for several years and keep the rest from watching a TV program or a movie. At the end of the experiment, you would know whether viewers' behavior is affected by television and films or whether it only reflects society's norms. Tavris and Offir (1977) refer to this experiment as "a psychologist's dream and a parents' nightmare."

We have now examined the influences of language and the media on sex-role stereotypes. How might we use this knowledge and information to improve our services to clients?

Implications for Client Services

There is not much we as providers of mental-health services can do to change the structure of the English language. Even if we tried to eliminate the pronouns used to differentiate men and women—for example, by changing "him" and "her" to something like "herm," or always using the pronoun "she" instead of "he" to mean people of unspecified sex—we would probably be creating more problems than we would solve. Nevertheless, we can be aware of the sex differences in language, and, especially in cases of mixed-sex groups, we can at least acknowledge the presence of both sexes by saying, for example, "Would each person please sign his or her name."

Our language usage can affect our services to our clients. Referring to our female clients as "ladies" or "girls" is not acceptable professional language and may be offensive to some clients. The patronizing use of phrases like "my dear" for women or younger clients is also totally unacceptable, even if the phrases are meant to express concern or empathy. Consider for a moment how you refer to your clients by name and how you prefer that they refer to you. Think about whether you are likely to refer to all clients by their first names or whether you tend more often to refer to children and women by their first names and to address men by their titles, such as Mr. Smith or Dr. Smith. Are you comfortable when clients address you by your first name, or would you prefer that they use your more formal title of Mr., Ms., or Dr.? Are you more comfortable when men address you by your first name than when women do, or do you feel the same in both cases? If you have discovered that you address men and women differently and/or accept or expect differences in the way they address you, you have probably been communicating sex-role biases to your clients. It doesn't really seem to matter whether you take a formal or an informal approach, as long as you treat both male and female clients the same and encourage clients of both sexes to refer to you the same way.

You should also be aware of any tendencies you might have to reinforce men and women or boys and girls differently for the ways they use language. For example, consider how you would respond if a woman stated, "He's a damn shit and a mean son-of-a bitch!" Compare your reaction to a man who stated the same thing. Would you react differently, either overtly or covertly, to swearing or "rough talk" from a man as compared to a woman? Would you yourself be more or less likely to use slang terms or to swear in the presence of either a woman or a man? Because of our sex-role expectations, many of us would have a stronger response, at least covertly, to a woman or girl who uses aggressive language, and we would be more likely to subtly or not so subtly reinforce her for using more "appropriate" language.

Whether or not you ever touch a client, touch is interpreted quite differently by most men and women. If you are a female clinician and touch a male client, he is, because of socialization expectations, likely to interpret the touch as having sexual connotations. If you touch a child or another woman, it may be considered "more appropriate" by the client, but it may also be interpreted as sexual or as "motherly" or patronizing. If you are a male clinician and touch a male client, he may have a very negative reaction because men are not used to being touched, especially by other men. On the other hand, if you touch a woman client, it may be interpreted as patronizing or as sexual, but the woman will probably not have a negative reaction unless she feels very threatened. Similarly, a male clinician who touches a child will usually be considered patronizing or "fatherly." The important issue is to be aware of your own feelings or justification for touching or not touching a client and to be aware of how touch is interpreted differently by different clients. Try to get in "touch" with your feelings about how you would react to various clients touching you. Do you like clients to touch you, or perhaps some clients and not others, or do you dislike being touched by any client at any time? You need to understand your own feelings and expectations before you can effectively help other people deal with theirs.

In mixed-sex group therapy, family therapy, or marriage counseling sessions, you as the therapist or cotherapist should be aware of the sex-role communication that is occurring among the members of the group as well as between cotherapists or therapists and the group members. Be aware of the tendency that women have to disqualify what they say by using "tag questions" or smiling inappropriately; and if you are a woman, be aware of these possible tendencies in yourself when you make interpretations or recommendations or simply participate in the group. Be aware of the tendency that men have to interrupt other people, especially women, and to control the topics of the discussion. Again, if you are a male, be aware of these possible tendencies in yourself. Whether you are a male or a female therapist, be aware of how the sexes use and interpret eye contact and requirements for personal space differently, and point out these behavior patterns and discuss them at appropriate times during the sessions.

As we discussed with language structure, there is little we can do as mental-health professionals to change the content of television programs or movies. At the same time, however, we can be aware of the influences of the media on our clients' lives as well as on our own lives, and we can use examples from TV and movies to teach our clients as well as our colleagues about the process of sex-role socialization. We can also, as professionals, protest verbally and in writing when a movie or television program or commercial is blatantly sex biased and detrimental to the well-being of children or adults of either sex. We must also continue to investigate through research the possible influences that the context of the media may be having on our society.

In the next chapter, we will examine how interest in the effects of sex-role socialization is leading to changes in attitudes about sex roles. We will also discuss how traditional sex-biased methods of evaluating the characteristics and interests of men and women are being replaced by less biased methods and materials.

3

Awareness and Change

Changes in Attitudes and Behavior

As people become aware of sex-role issues and become interested in the effects of sex roles on behavior, they also become increasingly dissatisfied with the existing prescribed roles for men and women. At the same time, however, stereotypes remain pervasive in our society, and there is little evidence to suggest that significant changes in behavior are accompanying the recent changes in attitudes.

An investigation comparing sex-role attitudes of undergraduate men and women (Osmond and Martin, 1975) indicates that both sexes accept a sexual division of labor within the family, with the woman continuing to have primary responsibility for the home and child care. Men and women disagree the most about sex-role changes involving women assuming supervisory, decision-making, and leadership roles outside of the family. Although men were not willing to accept women in these roles, the college women in this investigation indicated that women should be able to occupy such positions. The men did indicate that they would be more willing to accept smaller changes in women's roles, such as better jobs for women and better pay, as long as these changes did not become threatening to their own positions.

Other studies have reported similar findings regarding the differences in male and female attitudes toward changes in sex roles. The results indicate shifts away from traditional sex-role attitudes among college women, with increasing stress on their own achievement. Emphasis on the family role is still strong, but it is being considered in combination with achievement roles for women. College women seriously distrust "liberal" male attitudes and perceive that men want women to remain in their more traditional roles (Steinmann, 1975; Parelius, 1975). The reluctance of women to believe men when they indicate liberal attitudes about changes in sex roles is further reinforced by the results of an investigation in which men reported that their ideal woman would be extremely competent, successful, and adventurous—a virtual wonderwoman (O'Leary and Depner, 1975). The investigators concluded that the men were probably responding to the demand characteristics of the situation and overstating their beliefs in order to please the investigators and to avoid being labeled chauvinists, although it is possible that some men actually viewed this wonderwoman as ideal.

Only slight attitude changes are being reported in the research on sex-role change, and even in situations where attitudes do appear to be changing, the changes are usually not behaviorally observable. Some investigators have suggested that apparent trends toward attitude change among women may be the result of specific situational factors instead of significant changes in sex-role attitudes. In a study investigating sex-role attitudes of undergraduate college women, the subjects were required to describe themselves as conventional or nonconventional, in terms of female sex roles, to unobserved male partners. The subjects were given varied background information about their male partners that indicated either that the partner was attractive, athletic, unattached, and interested in meeting new women, or that he was not very attractive, had a girlfriend, was unathletic, and did not particularly want to meet other female college students. In addition to this information about the desirability of the partners, the subjects were also informed either that their partners had traditional views about women and wanted them to be home-oriented, passive, and concerned about their looks, or that the partner had less conventional views about women and preferred independent, ambitious, competitive women. The results of the study indicate that when the partner was "desirable," the women portrayed themselves as more or less conventional in terms of sex role, depending upon whether the partner's stereotyped view of women was traditional or nonconventional (Zanna and Pack, 1975). Apparently, rather than expressing their own feelings about sex-role stereotypes, these college women behaved in ways to confirm the expectations of the desirable men. The investigators concluded that some apparent sex-role changes in attitudes and behavior in women may indicate only that some women are trying to be what they perceive important men in their lives want them to be. Women may be responding to specific situational factors rather than changing attitudes and may actually be strengthening and reinforcing existing sex-role stereotypes by remaining dependent on the desires of men, even when it means not expressing their own views or not presenting accurate appraisals of themselves.

As long as women remain so greatly influenced by men's attitudes toward sex roles for women, it will be the fathers, brothers, husbands, and male lovers in our society who will continue to decide what roles a particular woman should pursue. If a man important to a woman expects her to be a good housewife and mother, she will be encouraged to shape her identity in these directions, whereas if he expects her to be achieving and intelligent, she will be encouraged to further her education and have employment outside of the home. Under these conditions, changes in specific sex-role requirements may occur, but the sex-role system will remain the same and equalitarian relationships between the sexes will not prevail.

In the majority of the studies investigating sex-role attitudes, college women appear to be the most liberal group studied. When other population samples are investigated, however, men consistently present themselves as more liberal than women about changing existing sex roles and stereotypes. Other variables besides sex reported to be associated with sex-role attitudes include levels of education, marital status, race, age, and employment. Liberal attitudes are reported more consistently by both men and women as their levels of education increase, and this variable appears to be especially powerful in influencing the views of women. The attitudes of younger men and women are apparently more liberal, and young black women, especially, report strong support for change. People who are married or widowed, especially housewives, tend to be less supportive of changes than single or divorced people of both sexes, and current employment for women is also associated with flexible sex-role attitudes (Chandler, 1973; Tavris, 1973).

Changes in Research Methods

Researchers on sex roles have tended to focus on the assumed differences between men and women while ignoring their similarities. Often women have been regarded as members of the "other," or different, sex, and investigators have attempted to categorize the ways that women deviate from male standards for behavior. Many women—as well as men—tend to believe that sex roles for women may have to change, but that roles for men should remain the same, since it is women who are different from men and who need to learn to adopt more masculine character traits. Rather than exploring whether, in fact, men and women are different, researchers have assumed that the differences are there and that only the extent of the differences needs to be assessed. Individual differences between members of the same sex have often been ignored in favor of global references to the behavior of "all" men versus "all" women.

Another factor that has reinforced identifying and classifying differences between the sexes and ignoring their similarities is that studies that identify significant sex differences are much more likely to be published in professional journals than studies that report nonsignificant ones. Research results that indicate there are no differences or only small differences in the behavior of men and women in specific situations are often not given enough emphasis or consideration. In some instances, as we noted in Chapter 1, when results indicating behavioral similarities have been reviewed in conjunction with studies that report behavioral differences, common assumptions about sex differences have been shown to be completely unfounded (Maccoby and Jacklin, 1974).

Masculinity and Femininity

One of the major approaches to the study of sex differences has been the assessment of the masculinity and femininity of individuals. In this approach, masculinity and femininity are assumed to be the opposite ends of a single continuum and to be inversely correlated, so that if a person is more masculine, he or she automatically becomes less feminine. Masculinity is usually defined by primarily instrumental behavior characteristics, such as assertiveness, independence, and self-confidence, whereas femininity is typically defined by primarily expressive behavior characteristics, such as nurturance, sensitivity, and emotionality. The major criticism of this approach is that it categorizes an individual as either "masculine" or "feminine," but it does not allow for sex-role flexibility. An individual is forced to choose between two alternatives and is not allowed to combine characteristics of both sexes. The existence of an individual to which neither of these labels applies is usually never considered or is ignored. Another problem with this approach is that research has demonstrated that a person's masculinity or femininity score can be affected by numerous variables and that these traits are not always stable and enduring. As educational level increases, women become more "masculine" according to standard M-F scales, and men become more "feminine." Differences in masculinity and femininity are also associated with age, and even geographical location is apparently related to masculinity and femininity scores (Constantinople, 1973). Therefore, the conceptualization of masculinity and femininity as comprehensive, enduring, mutually exclusive traits has not been supported by research evidence.

Newer Approaches to Research

Within recent years, psychologists have proposed two-dimensional schemes to remedy some of these research problems. In the newer approaches, masculinity and femininity are assumed to be two different dimensions instead of continuous traits, so that an individual can have both masculine and feminine characteristics. Spence et al. have developed a "dualistic approach to psychological masculinity and femininity" (Spence and Helmreich, 1978). Their research results clearly demonstrate that masculinity and femininity do not relate negatively to each other and that a "dualistic" rather than a "bipolar" conception of these two psychological dimensions is most appropriate. Rather than assuming, for example, that aggressiveness is assigned only to men and nurturance is assigned only to women, in the dualistic approach a man or a woman can be both aggressive and nurturant or can have neither of these characteristics. In earlier research questionnaires (for example, Rosenkrantz et al., 1968) men and women were assigned characteristics from bipolar, forced-choice scales (e.g., "not at all aggressive"—"very aggressive," "not at all emotional"—"very emotional") and then on the basis of their total scores were assigned the labels of either "masculine" or "feminine." In the dualistic approach, men and women rate themselves and others on the "Personnel Attributes Questionnaire" (PAQ), which consists of a series of five-point traits believed to differentiate the sexes. This questionnaire is divided into three separate scales, including masculinity (M), femininity (F), and masculinity-femininity (M-F), and is scored so that subjects can be classified into *four* separate categories. These scores include a "masculine" score, a "feminine" score, and two scores that combine attributes considered both masculine and feminine (Spence et al., 1974, 1975) (see Table 3.1).

Psychologist Sandra Bem has used the term "androgyny" to define the ability to behave in ways traditionally associated with both sexes. Androgyny comes from two Greek words: *andros*, meaning man, and *gyne*, meaning woman; an androgynous person is one who combines masculine and feminine behavior. Androgyny also usually implies flexibility of sex roles and the ability to change behavior in different situations. Because they have no sex-role images to maintain, androgynous individuals can engage in whatever behavior seems most effective, regardless of whether it is stereotyped as appropriate for either men or women. Androgynous people have a wider range of capabilities, and depending upon what the specific situation requires, can show assertiveness or warmth and can be equally effective in both situations (Bem, 1972).

In research that has paralleled the work of Spence et al., Bem (1974) has developed a questionnaire called the Bem Sex-Role Inventory (BSRI). Specifically, the BSRI consists of twenty "mas-

Table 3.1.
Scoring Categories for the Personal Attributes Questionnaire and the Bem Sex-Role Inventory.

		Masculinity	
		High	Low
Femininity	High	Androgynous	Feminine
	Low	Masculine	Undifferentiated

culine" personality characteristics, such as ambitious, self-reliant, and assertive; twenty "feminine" personality characteristics, such as affectionate, gentle, and understanding; and twenty "neutral" characteristics, such as happy, conceited, and truthful. The BSRI asks subjects to indicate on a seven-point scale how well each of sixty personality characteristics describes them. On the basis of the responses, each person receives a "masculinity" score, a "femininity" score, and an "androgyny" score. If the person's "masculinity" score is significantly higher than the "femininity" score, the person has a masculine sex-role identity, and if the person's "femininity" score is significantly higher than the "masculinity" score, the person has a feminine sex-role identity. If, on the other hand, both "masculinity" and "femininity" scores are high and approximately equal, the person has an androgynous sex-role identity. Bem originally indicated that both high and low scores would indicate androgyny if the scores were approximately equal, but subsequent research has suggested that low scores on both the masculinity and femininity scales indicate an "undifferentiated" sex-role identity rather than an androgynous one (Spence et al., 1975).

Research Based on the Dualistic Approach

In *Masculinity and Femininity,* Spence and Helmreich (1978) report research results that indicate that the dualistic conception is valid for groups of people who differ in age, socioeconomic status, and geographic location. They found that although many individuals are "appropriately" sex-typed (i.e., men high in masculinity and low in femininity and women the reverse), many other men and women are androgynous (high in both masculine and feminine characteristics) and others are high in neither (undifferentiated).

In addition to the Personal Attributes Questionnaire, Spence et al. have also developed several other self-report instruments that they have used in their research. The "Attitudes Toward Women Scale" (Spence et al., 1972, 1973) is a questionnaire for assessing attitudes about the rights, roles, and privileges that women "ought" to have or should be "permitted" to have within our society. The "Texas Social Behavior Inventory" (Helmreich and Stapp, 1974) measures self-esteem and is designed to assess an individual's self-confidence and competence in social situations, and the "Parental Attitudes Questionnaire" was developed to measure men's and women's assessment of their parents' attitudes and behaviors and the family atmosphere (Spence and Helmreich, 1978).

Using these instruments in investigations with both high school and college students, Spence et al. found highly significant differences in self-esteem in both sexes for the four PAQ categories. The highest self-esteem was reported by androgynous students, followed by the masculine, feminine, and undifferentiated, respectively. For both high school and college students, correlations between attitudes toward women and the four categories tended to be in the same direction as for self-esteem, but the correlations were low and not always significant, and the investigators maintain that these results indicate that masculine and feminine attributes are not strongly related to abstract attitudes about acceptable sex roles for women.

Strong relationships were found between the students' reports of their masculine and feminine characteristics and their perceptions of their parents' characteristics and childrearing attitudes and behavior. Overall, students from homes in which both parents are perceived as androgynous are most likely to report highest self-esteem and social competence, and those with undifferentiated parents report the least self-esteem and confidence. Following the androgynous parents, the most "healthy" home atmospheres were perceived in homes where the parent combinations were androgynous father-feminine mother, masculine father-androgynous mother, and masculine father-feminine mother, respectively. "Unhealthy" home atmospheres resulted when either or both of the parents were perceived as undifferentiated or when the feminine father-masculine mother pattern was perceived.

For male students, the results suggest a strong association between sons' and the fathers' characteristics with the contribution of the mother being less critical. For women, the influence of the parents was more nearly equal.

Research Based on Bem's Concept of Androgyny

Utilizing the BSRI, Bem et al. designed a series of investigations to test the hypothesis that psychologically androgynous individuals would be more likely than high masculine, high feminine, or sex-reversed individuals to display sex-role adaptability and flexibility across situations. Two experiments with college students provide support for this hypothesis (Bem, 1975).

The first of these experiments was constructed to determine whether masculine and androgynous subjects would remain more independent from social pressure than feminine subjects. Volunteer undergraduate students, nine masculine, nine feminine, and nine androgynous subjects of each sex, as identified by the BSRI, were solicited for an experiment on humor and were told that the experiment would consist of rating cartoons for funniness. Subjects were run in groups but were placed in soundproofed cubicles where they believed they could hear each other's ratings. What the subjects actually were hearing were prerecorded tapes of voices which all agreed that a cartoon was funny when it was not or that it was not funny when it was. For each cartoon, the subjects were asked to give their ratings after hearing two other false ratings. As predicted, both male and female high masculine and androgynous subjects conformed on fewer trials than male and female high feminine subjects, and masculine and androgynous subjects did not differ from one another in amount of conformity.

The second experiment was designed to test the hypothesis that both feminine and androgynous subjects, as identified on the BSRI, would be more nurturant than masculine subjects. Men and women undergraduates were solicited for an experiment on "mood" and then were run through the experiment individually. First, in order to equalize their moods, subjects were given the task of building something with geometrical disks. Next, a kitten was brought into the room, and the subjects were instructed to interact with the kitten in any way they wished. After this, subjects played a challenging game of skill. And then the kitten was returned to the room and the subjects were instructed to do anything that they wished for ten minutes. The results for the men confirmed the original hypothesis: Feminine and androgynous men did not differ significantly from one another, and both were significantly more responsive to the kitten than the masculine men. Although, as predicted, the androgynous women were also very responsive to the kitten, the feminine women, contrary to the hypothesis, were significantly less responsive to the kitten and the masculine women fell ambiguously in between.

Considering these two experiments together, it appears that androgynous subjects of both sexes display a high level of independence when under stress—typically considered a "male" characteristic—and display a high level of nurturance when given the opportunity to interact with a kitten—typically considered "feminine" behavior. The masculine men display independence but not nurturance, and the feminine men display nurturance but not independence. The masculine women display greater independence than the feminine women, but they only displayed a moderate amount of nurturance. The feminine women appeared to be the most restricted and were not only low in independence but were also low in nurturance. Consequently, the feminine women appeared to have the most serious behavior deficits.

Bem et al. have investigated the effects and influences of androgyny in several additional studies (Bem, 1976). In an investigation following the two experiments with conformity and nurturance, male and female subjects were left alone with a five-month-old baby for ten minutes and observed through a one-way mirror. One of the hypotheses being tested was that high feminine women would respond with a high level of nurturance to a human infant, even though they had been inhibited with or fearful of a small kitten. Feminine and androgynous men were more responsive to the baby than masculine men. However, there were no significant differences among the women, and feminine, androgynous and masculine women were all equally affectionate toward the baby.

The feminine women were eventually found to be responsive and nurturant in a study which required them to be responsive listeners. It appears that the feminine women may be overly concerned about the possible negative consequences of their behavior in any situation where they are required to take the initiative and that these women withdraw or engage in as little behavior as possible unless they are placed in a secure situation where they are only required to respond to the actions or to the words of other people.

Other Relevant Research

A review of relevant literature indicates that men and women who are less sex typed and who demonstrate more flexible behavior are generally higher in intelligence and show more creativity than men and women who are strongly sex typed (Maccoby, 1966). In addition, high femininity has been found to be associated with high anxiety, low social acceptance, and, in general, poorer adjustment for women; and it has not been demonstrated that high masculinity, except during adolescence, always enhances adjustment for males. Research also indicates that both men and women classified as androgynous tend to receive more awards during their school years, date more, and experience sickness less often than highly sex-typed people (Spence, Helmreich, and Stapp, 1975).

In support of the conclusions reached by Spence et al., other investigators have noted that androgynous people tend to have different home backgrounds than people who are highly sex typed. The parents of androgynous men and women tend to be less stereotyped in their own definitions of masculinity and femininity and to offer a wider range of behavioral and attitudinal possibilities to their children. Mothers are apparently relatively achievement oriented, yet at the same time they obtain satisfaction from maternal and marital roles. Fathers tend to be respected and successful men, but they are at the same time able to share decision making and financial management with their wives. The parental relationship is relatively satisfying and free of conflict, and both parents are usually psychologically healthy. Both parents of androgynous people provide models of warmth, competence, encouragement, consideration, and sharing of responsibility for their children (Kelly and Worell, 1976). Many high feminine and high masculine people, on the other hand, apparently grow up in families where there is clear and conventional role differentiation between the parents; and people who are sex-reversed—that is, identifying strongly with femininity when they are men and identifying strongly with masculinity when they are women—often come from families characterized by conflict and psychopathology (Block, von der Lippe, and Block, 1973).

We have now examined how awareness of sex-role issues and changes in attitudes about sex roles have affected research methods and questionnaires. Before we turn our attention to the issues and problems of test biases in other kinds of assessment and diagnostic instruments, let us first look at some of the implications of these changes.

Implications for Mental-Health Services

As social scientists and mental-health professionals, we are probably more aware of sex-role issues than almost any other group of people in our society. We know that attitudes about sex roles and stereotypes are changing, especially for women, and we see evidence of these changing attitudes in our research and from our clients, as well as in the publicity about the women's liberation movement, the campaign for the Equal Rights Amendment, and the popularity of women's studies programs on most college campuses. At the same time, however, we are aware, while many other people in society are not, that these changes in attitudes are not being reflected in widespread changes in behavior. Although many people, including some of our colleagues, are paying lip service to the idea of more liberal and flexible sex roles for women and for men, stereotyped behavior is still pervasive. Even when behavior does appear to be changing, especially for young women, the changes may often be deceptive and may be occurring only temporarily to impress other people.

When providing services to clients, we need to be cautious about projecting our own attitudes onto them and assuming they are ready to change their behavior because they are aware of sex-role issues. At the same time, we need to be aware of our own sex-role biases and keep ourselves from preventing or not reinforcing behavior changes when the client is ready for them.

The clients who are most likely to be aware of the effects of sex-role stereotypes and are most flexible in their behavior are young, black, employed, college-educated women who are single or divorced. Even a client who has all of these characteristics, however, may not desire to change her sex-role status. Each client must be treated as an individual rather than as a man or a woman, and therapists need to be aware that there are more differences between men and other men, and women and other women, than between men as a group and women as a group.

The research on masculinity and femininity has shown that many mental-health professionals have been in error for years in assuming that the most "masculine" men and the most "feminine" women are the healthiest people in our society. We now know that "high feminine" women may be the most restricted and poorly adjusted of all groups within our society, while "androgynous" people of both sexes appear to be the most flexible and well-adjusted. Instead of reinforcing "appropriate" sex roles for our clients, we will be providing them with much better service by teaching them and reinforcing them for androgynous behavior.

Think about your own behavior characteristics and estimate whether your score on the Personal Attributes Questionnaire or the Bem Sex-Role Inventory would indicate that you are sex-typed (masculine for men, feminine for women), androgynous (high masculine and high feminine for both sexes), cross-sexed (feminine for men, masculine for women) or undifferentiated (low masculine and low feminine for both sexes). Many of you have probably estimated that you are androgynous and a few of you may be correct, but most of you are probably sex-typed. Cross-sexed people are a small minority in most groups (Meerdink and Schmitt, 1977), and it is unlikely that many undifferentiated people would be capable of becoming mental-health-service providers. For your own interest and personal awareness and as a check as to how well you are in touch with your own values and sex-role preferences, refer to Appendix A, Table II, in *Masculinity and Femininity* (Spence and Helmreich, 1978) and complete and score the Personal Attribute Questionnaire, or obtain and self-administer a copy of the BSRI. You may be surprised at the results.

The PAQ and BSRI, as well as the Attitudes Toward Women Scale and the Parental Attitudes Questionnaire, are especially important research instruments because they were developed specifically to eliminate the sex biases and sex-role stereotypes that have characterized previous questionnaires. Other popular and widely used tests have been found to contain sex biases, and many of these are in the process of being revised or new instruments are being developed to replace them. We will now turn our attention to a discussion of test bias.

Test Bias

We have examined the ways that sex bias can affect questionnaires and test inventories that view the concepts of masculinity and femininity as opposites or mutually exclusive. Consistent sex biases have also been found as well in several mental-health diagnostic tests and interest inventories.

According to Garai (1970), many available mental-health tests fail to take into consideration the different effects of the socialization process for the two sexes. For example, the tests assume that women and men derive happiness and satisfaction from similar experiences and that their unhappiness is caused by similar worries and frustrations. In addition, the tests assume that men and women share the same needs and life goals and that they do not basically differ in attitudes or values. Garai maintains that there is a male bias inherent in tests traditionally used to diagnose mental health and that there should be different criteria established for the evaluation of mental health.

Definitions of Test Bias

In an article entitled "The Many Definitions of Test Bias," Flaugher (1978) states that there are many different possible definitions of test bias and that we, as mental-health professionals, continually run the risk of losing perspective on the issue by looking for only one, or the "real," issue of test bias.

According to Flaugher, part of the problem stems from the incorrect usage of the words "achievement" and "aptitude" to apply to certain tests. Even though correlations between these two kinds of tests are frequently positive and the contents of these tests frequently overlap, tests measuring achievement and tests measuring aptitude are not meant to be interpreted in the same way. An achievement-test score means that a course of instruction has been learned successfully or unsuccessfully and further educational instruction in that particular area is either necessary or unnecessary. An aptitude score, on the other hand, indicates whether or not the individual has the ability and the potential necessary for accomplishment. Flaugher maintains that the distinction between the interpretation of achievement and aptitude also has great social significance. If achievement scores are low, educational programs will be under pressure to improve that achievement. If aptitude scores are low, however, educational resources may justifiably be withdrawn. Society is pressured to assume greater responsibility for achievement failure than aptitude failure, and confusion over the proper interpretation of test scores can lead to very emotional reactions among the people affected by the scores as well as in the general public. For example, if a test is represented as an achievement test and most men do well on the test and most women do poorly, the women will protest, and often with just cause, that the test was unfair because it asked questions that were easier for men to answer, or it was not an accurate appraisal of what the women had learned, and/or the educational process was biased toward men. On the other hand, if the test is represented as an aptitude test to determine whether or not an individual has sufficient capacity to achieve in a particular occupational field or course of endeavor, it is at least possible that higher scores for men and lower scores for some women might be reflecting more basic sex differences in aptitude, such as in mathematical ability or verbal-spatial skills.

A tendency toward overinterpretation of test results can also result in test bias. Tests are frequently named for the kinds of tasks they include rather than for what they were originally intended to measure (Ebel, 1976). For example, a test that asks people to make suggestions or offer opinions may be called a test of "creativity," and a test that requires people to answer questions and solve mathematical problems may be called a test of "intelligence." Since we can't measure all aspects of creativity or intelligence, we concentrate on those things that can be measured and then consider them as all-important. In reality, these aspects comprise only a narrow portion of the spectrum and most likely those aspects are related to academic opportunities.

The particular content of tests is also often biased. The test language has almost always reflected the sex bias inherent in the English language, as we noted in Chapter 2. As Flaugher notes, tests may not be any more guilty of sex bias than other sources of language, but they are an appropriate medium through which social changes can be accomplished. As we mentioned previously, it is also imperative that professionals using tests be aware of this issue. Test content may also be biased if it contains questions that are "unfair" to a given segment of society. The public interpretation of "fair" seems to be that fair tests give one the opportunity to indicate all of the information one has and "unfair" tests fail to ask questions that one could have answered and consequently fail to reveal all of the strengths that one possesses. The problem with this definition is that it is impossible to develop a test that asks all of the "right" questions for all people. A number of attempts have been made to eliminate items from tests that are "unfair" to particular subgroups within society (Bianchini, 1976; Flaugher, 1974), but the results have been generally inconclusive and disappointing. Considering the importance of testing, such research should be continued, but except for changes in sexist language, there is more involved in test bias than simply asking the "wrong" questions.

Gulliksen (1976) suggests that some test bias might be eliminated by examining the popular criterion measures we use. For example, do grade-point averages accurately predict future college performance for women and men, or do ratings by supervisors accurately reflect competence for future promotions? Problems with criterion measures have been the source of many legal disputes, especially when there is a question whether the criterion measures the same thing for two or more groups. The legal disputes usually concern the right of the school or employer to establish its own standards for interpreting the results of the tests or evaluations used. In other words, should everyone be evaluated equally or should quota systems be used that may be biased for or against women and/or other minority groups?

Other possible sources of test bias suggested by Flaugher (1978) include selection variables—for example, using paper-and-pencil tests as compared to structured interviews or past academic records—and the testing atmosphere. If people taking tests feel out of place or unwelcome in the test setting, it is only reasonable to expect their performance to be less than optimal. Similarly, women and men may not perform equally well on written tests, especially since women as a group tend to score better than men as a group in verbal ability, and it might be fairer for both sexes to establish tests that include samples of several types of behavior rather than just one. Flaugher concludes that it is important to keep in mind all of the various definitions of test bias, even though the general public continues to see only a single issue.

There are biases inherent in many tests used to diagnose mental health (Garai, 1970) as well as in the instruments used to evaluate vocational interests and career development. A number of investigators have pointed out that interest tests are often biased (Harmon, 1973; Tittle, 1974), and the problem of biases in the materials used in vocational counseling is one that merits our attention.

Bias in Vocational Counseling Materials

Since interest inventories are a crucial part of vocational counseling, vocational counselors must evaluate these inventories to determine whether or not they are free from restricting influences. Counselors, both women and men, are often unaware of the sexual bias inherent in the major inventories as presently constructed. When investigators (Schlossberg and Pietrofesa, 1978) asked trained counselors whether or not they believed that the two most widely used interest inventories, the Strong Vocational Interest Blank and the Kuder Occupational Interest Survey, were biased, only a minority of the men and women counselors believed that they were. According to the investigators, the majority of the counselors were amazed by the presentation of a detailed description of the biases inherent in each test, even though the results of several previous investigations had indicated the presence of sex bias in these instruments.

Schlossberg and Goodman (1972) have pointed out four major limitations of the Strong Vocational Interest Blank: (1) The Strong includes thirty-three occupations for men that are not listed for women, such as author, psychiatrist, and journalist. It also includes thirty-seven occupations listed only for women, such as elementary school teacher and medical technologist. (2) When the same person completes both the form for men and the form for women, the profiles turn out differently. For example, a woman may score highly as a dental assistant or as a physical therapist on the women's form but score highly as a potential physician or psychologist on the men's form. Or, a man might score highly as a potential registered nurse or dental assistant on the women's form and also score highly as a potential guidance counselor or personnel director on the men's form. (3) The current manual which offers guidelines to counselors states that many young women do not have strong occupational interests and may only obtain high scores in certain "premarital" occupations, such as elementary school teacher or secretary! (4) The use of the Strong may be attacked on legal grounds since it is so clearly sex biased.

Other investigators have published dozens of articles condemning the Strong and other counseling materials for having separate forms for women and men, separate norms, and separate profiles for each sex (Frazier and Sadker, 1973), as well as providing a more restricted range of occupations for women than for men (Tittle, 1974).

Schlossberg and Pietrofesa (1978) maintain that an equally biased picture becomes apparent in almost all guidance materials, including the "Occupational Outlook Handbook," the "Dictionary of Occupational Titles," career brochures, and college catalogues. If the information contained in any of these materials reflects stereotyped roles for men and women or recommends that the sexes be treated differently, the materials are sex biased. For example, the opening paragraph in the American College Testing (ACT) Program's brochure describing their career-planning program contains such statements as: "Care should be used in interpreting predictions for a student of one sex in a program in which the other sex predominates" (American College Testing, 1971).

Changes to Eliminate Bias

The Strong Vocational Interest Blank (as well as other widely used interest inventories) is currently being revised in an attempt to eliminate sexual bias. At the same time, new instruments are being developed to replace older sex-biased inventories. For example, the brochure for the Jackson Vocational Interest Survey (1978) claims that the JVIS places equal emphasis upon the measurements and interests of men and women and that the instrument was standardized so that an equal number of men and women contributed to the selection of the items and the scales. In addition, the format is supposed to allow men and women to be measured in terms of a common set of interest dimensions instead of discriminating between the so-called "male" and "female" occupations. Other examples of tests and career information that are described as designed to eliminate sex bias are the Strong-Campbell Interest Inventory (Campbell, 1973) and the Crites Career Maturity Inventory (Crites, 1973).

Dewey (1977) has reported developing a new technique called the Non-Sexist Vocational Card Sort which removes a client from the traditional paper-and-pencil interest inventories and, according to Dewey, enables the counselor to make interpretations based on the client's behavior as well as on his or her self-reported interests. The same seventy-six vocational alternatives are offered to men and women, and the gender of the occupational titles has been neutralized. For example, clergyman has been changed to clergyperson, and airline stewardess to steward/stewardess. The format is designed to encourage exploration of sex-role biases, and the counselor is an active participant in the process. The client is instructed to put the cards into three categories, including "Might Choose," "Would Not Choose," and "In Question" and then is encouraged to explain his or her choices. The counselor directs the activity and notes the behavior and comments that the client makes during the process. The client and counselor then plan together additional steps the client should follow to gather more data about the areas in which she or he is most interested. Dewey describes her approach as a structured interview technique that generates a wealth of data and at the same time frees counselors from the necessity of relying on computer printouts.

We are now aware of some of the sex biases inherent in almost all test materials and in vocational-counseling materials in particular. What are some of the implications of our discussion for vocational guidance and testing?

Implications for Client Services

If we, as mental-health-service providers, decided that we wouldn't use any sex-biased tests, we would be hard pressed to find any tests to use and could end up using no instruments at all. Projective tests are probably the least offensive in terms of test construction, but even with projective tests, bias may be introjected into the procedure by the examiner, especially if any established criteria for interpretation are used (Rawlings and Carter, 1977).

Rather than go to the extreme of giving up testing completely, however, chances are that most of us will continue to use testing as part of our services to our clients whether we are clinicians using the tests for diagnostic purposes, guidance counselors using the tests for vocational guidance services, or employment managers using the tests for selection and placement purposes.

Those of us who continue to use tests must become aware that the concept of norm groups is inherently conservative and can serve as a barrier to change. As long as we try to fit people into established norms, we will be encouraging the continuation of sex biases for both women and men.

We can make an effort to use less sex-biased instruments like the ones described in this chapter or projective tests, but at the same time we have to become aware of biases within ourselves as well as in the materials we use. For example, what about the woman client who does *not* express a nontraditional career choice when test and interview data suggest that a career would be realistic for her? Would you explore her reasons for making a traditional sex-typed choice instead of a nontraditional one and suggest a wider selection of options? What about the client who does select a nontraditional career? Would you subtly discourage him or her, or would you help the client learn more about the procedures for pursuing such a career? Awareness of bias is not sufficient by itself but must be accompanied by corrective action if we are to provide effective services (Oliver, 1975).

Changing the content of the Strong or the Kuder will not automatically change a client's self-image and the limits he or she has internalized. Counselors and other service providers must become aware of the fact that career guidance, especially for women, must take place within a life-planning context. Too narrow an approach that emphasizes only the content of the specific occupation chosen will not meet the needs of women who have not been socially reinforced to think in terms of life planning for roles other than those of wife and mother.

Test biases have been particularly oppressive for women but also restrictive for men, and although there has been an awareness of the issues concerning test biases for many years, progress on updating tests or discarding the most biased of the tests has been slow. Dewey (1977) places at least part of the blame on test authors and publishers who have an economic advantage in maintaining the status quo. Investigators who disagree with this position, however, state that while some of the apparent sex biases may result from inadequacies in test construction, others can be described as "unavoidable" consequences of the different "nature" of male and female interests in our present society (Wirtenberg and Nakamura, 1976). Also, some are of the opinion that if taking inventories has any effect at all, it is in the direction of widening the options for girls and focusing the options for boys (Holland, 1974).

As mental-health professionals, we must weigh the evidence (and the overwhelming evidence is that some tests are definitely sex biased), be very aware of related sex-role issues, and try to provide our clients with services that are sex-biased as little as possible. We must be aware of the influences that our own behavior as examiners can have on testing situations and outcomes, and, when feasible, engage in appropriate action to eliminate testing biases by, for instance, refusing to use biased materials or by helping to develop awareness among colleagues and trainees.

In the next chapter we will focus our attention on sex-role issues in the areas of intelligence and achievement. Also, with these issues in mind, we will continue our discussion of test bias.

4

Intelligence and Achievement

Sex Differences in Intelligence

Historically, one of the most popular explanations for the differences in behavior and in status of the sexes has been that women are less intelligent than men. In an article entitled "Functionalism, Darwinism, and the Psychology of Women: A Study in Social Myth," Stephanie Shields (1975) has explored the pervasiveness of this belief throughout history and has reviewed three of the major theories that were devised to "prove" male intellectual superiority. According to Shields, the "woman question" was first conceptualized as a social question rather than as a scientific one. The function of women was considered only in relation to men and was thought of as different from the function of men but complementary. Since the nineteenth century, when the issue of female intelligence finally became a subject for scientific study rather than an accepted "fact" of nature, three major areas of investigation have included: (1) structural differences in the brains of men and women and the implications of these differences for intelligence and temperament, (2) greater variability in male behavior, and (3) the concept of maternal instinct and its effect on female intelligence and temperament.

Brain Size

Although it had long been believed that women's brains were "imperfect" and inferior to those of men, it wasn't until the beginning of the nineteenth century that researchers hypothesized that various mental and moral abilities were located in specific areas of the brain surface. "Cranioscopy," or the examination of the external skull and head area to detect deficiencies, became a popular "scientific" endeavor, and, as Shields notes, the researchers fully anticipated that sex differences explaining the inferior intelligence of women would be discovered. Some investigators maintained that the quality of intelligence was proportional to relative brain size. For example, since most women have smaller heads than most men, this was considered "proof" of the differences between male and female intelligence. In other words, the bigger the brain the better the brain. Other investigators contended that the presence of certain mental abilities was dependent upon the development of corresponding brain areas or centers. For example, when it was noted that the frontal lobes of men's brains tended to be larger than the frontal lobes of women's brains, it was believed that the frontal lobes were the centers for intellectual abilities and other areas of the brain were the centers for temperament and emotions. When the ratio of brain weight to body weight was computed, it was found that women have a proportionally larger brain than men. Therefore, this ratio was considered less important than the ratio of brain surface to body surface, which favors men.

As you might suspect, more recent studies of brain size (Elliott, 1969) have demonstrated that there is a large margin of error when estimating brain sizes, and brains differing as much as 15 percent in size have been found in heads that are externally the same size. Also, the development of the frontal lobes, once considered an indicator of intellectual abilities in men, is now considered less important than other areas of the brain. The controversy concerning the importance of brain size and brain areas as indicators of intelligence diminished when tests of intellectual functioning were developed. Nevertheless, the belief in differences between men's and women's use of their brains or reasoning abilities is still apparent, even though the language used is no longer as primitive as "more brain means better brain."

The Variability Hypothesis

The second major hypothesis reviewed by Shields is the "variability hypothesis," or the belief that men have the potential for a wider range of possible behavior than women. This notion has been popular for centuries. The ancient Greeks thought heat and dryness were characteristic of men, and moisture and coolness were characteristic of women. Since they believed dryness of spirit was necessary for intelligence, they naturally believed that men were more intelligent than women. The maintenance of dryness and heat was thought to be the function of the testicles, and if a man was castrated, the effects were thought to be the same as if his brain had been damaged directly (Huarte, 1959). Although many men today would still feel as threatened by the thought of castration, we no longer believe that, at least in most cases, the testicles control a man's intelligence.

Although the theory of evolution as originally proposed by Darwin did not specify differences in intellectual capacities for men and women, his theory has been interpreted and extended by others to "prove" that women are inferior to men. Darwin had proposed that variation from the norm was the mechanism for evolutionary process. Therefore, people who are "different" from other people are the progressive members of the human species. Investigators documented more frequent occurrences of physical deformities among men and a higher incidence of mental deficiency or retardation among men. They also found, not unexpectedly, that there are greater numbers of men who are considered to be or to have been geniuses or to have achieved "eminence." The rationale for the variability hypothesis is that since women *have* not excelled, they therefore *cannot* excel; and although men are more likely than women to be retarded or deformed, this variability in the range of their potential behavior actually makes them the superior sex, because they are also the ones who will have the highest intelligence and the strongest bodies and minds. The female range of intelligence was thought to be relatively narrow, limiting a woman's intelligence to an average level and limiting her expertise to practical rather than abstract life situations.

In the United States, the variability hypothesis was influential in the testing movement and was often used to "prove" that educational opportunities for women and men, if they were available to women at all, should be separate and different in order to qualify women for the practical purposes of life and men for the more difficult pursuits. Although a few educators questioned the "natural" roles for each sex and maintained that what appeared as intellectual inferiority in women was actually the result of the socialization process (Mill, 1955), most educators felt that it was their obligation to teach and foster passivity and dependency in girls and women. According to Shields' review, one of the most influential people to endorse the variability hypotheses was Edward Thorndike, a pioneer in the American testing movement, who maintained that because the range of female ability was so narrow, the talents of the "few" gifted women should be channeled into fields where they were most needed, such as nursing or teaching. He also maintained that our educators should be aware that most women would be restricted to mediocre levels of ability and achievement.

A small but persistent minority, mainly women, challenged the variability hypothesis. Leta Hollingworth, a colleague of Thorndike at Columbia University, actively investigated the variability hypothesis. She argued that what prevented women from becoming eminent achievers was their *social* role in a country where constraints were placed upon their education and employment by law as well as custom. Furthermore, she maintained that the true potential of women could only be discovered by allowing them the opportunities to choose a career and/or marriage and motherhood. Her arguments sound much like those of many contemporary social scientists, even though she was publishing her views in 1914 and 1916. Even today the variability hypothesis has not been totally disproved, and in fact, some investigators view it as a plausible explanation for sex differences (Heim, 1970; Hutt, 1972). Nevertheless, according to Shields (1974), variation within each sex is so much greater than variation between the sexes that the "meaning" of the variability hypothesis is "trivial."

Maternal Instinct

The third hypothesis reviewed in Shields' article concerns the belief that women, as a direct consequence of their reproductive physiology, will instinctively abandon intellectual pursuits in order to adequately bear and nurture children. Differences in structure between men and women are assumed to imply differences in abilities, temperament, and intelligence. As "energy" is used for maternal activities, there is less "energy" available for the development of other qualities; or, as Shields interprets this, a woman is thought to be, in essence, a stunted man. Thorndike believed that the tendency to display maternal concerns was universal among women and maintained that even if the environments for boys and girls were absolutely similar, instincts would produce definite and important differences between the mental abilities of the two sexes (Thorndike, 1914).

In the 1920s, behaviorists such as J. B. Watson (1926) became very critical of the concept of instincts and emphasized instead the influences of society on men's and women's successful role performance. The behaviorists concentrated on defining universal laws of behavior, and the study of differences between women and men was neglected until the publication of Freud's psychoanalytic theory in the mid-1930s revived interest.

As Shields concludes, the fate of the issues of brain size, variability and maternal instinct in contemporary social science is less important than the recognition of the role they have played and are still playing: the role of social myth. All of the various hypotheses, whether they were disproved or not, have reinforced the belief in differences between the sexes in intelligence. Since Einstein's name was Albert and not Alice, people have continued to assume that women cannot be geniuses, and of the women who *have* attained recognition for their intellectual abilities, some have had to work under assumed male names. For example, Aurore Dudevant wrote under the pen name of George Sand, and Mary Ann Evans was better known as George Eliot (O'Leary, 1977).

Although there is no evidence that women and men differ in average intelligence, consistent sex differences have been found in comparative studies of verbal, visual-spatial, and mathematical abilities (Maccoby and Jacklin, 1974; Unger and Denmark, 1975).

We will now take a closer look at these areas of sex differences and review some of the theories that have been formulated to explain them.

Verbal Abilities

When social scientists speak of verbal abilities they are referring to specific measurable abilities including the use of vocabulary, the ability to name objects, fluency, and the use of correct grammar, as well as more complex abilities such as creative writing, reading comprehension, and the use of language in logical reasoning. Consistent sex differences in verbal ability do not appear until late childhood or adolescence, and then girls begin to outperform boys and continue to outperform them on measures of verbal ability throughout high school and college (Maccoby and Jacklin, 1974).

One possible explanation for the greater verbal abilities of women is based on the hypothesis that mothers of girls provide a richer language environment for their daughters than do the mothers of boys (Cherry and Lewis, 1976). The results of several studies indicate that mothers vocalize more to daughters than to sons, and infant girls have been found to be more responsive to their mothers' vocalizations (Lewis and Freedle, 1973). At the same time, however, other investigations have not found differences in language abilities for preschool boys and girls (Koenigsknecht and Friedman, 1976). Some of the alternatives to the environmental explanation for superior verbal abilities in women focus on biological differences between women and men. Investigators Buffery and Gray (1972) have suggested that since girls are developmentally ahead of boys at birth and for several years thereafter, their brains mature at a faster rate than boys' brains. Specifically, it is the left hemisphere of the brain that is the major location of the language function. According to these investigators, girls are developmentally ahead of boys in attaining left-hemisphere dominance and therefore, throughout life, maintain greater verbal facility because language was developed at an earlier age. Other investigations have not supported this hypothesis, however (Landsell, 1976; McGlone, 1976). Other biologically based explanations have focused on the possibility that the female sex hormone, estrogen, facilitates the learning of verbal skills (Hutt, 1972).

Why women outperform men on tasks of verbal ability is an exceedingly complex issue, and there are many competing explanations and contradictory findings. It leads directly to another complex question: Why, if girls and women have higher verbal abilities than men, aren't there more creative and skillful women authors and writers participating in relevant occupations? What happens to most gifted women during the socialization process that keeps them from developing and utilizing their superior verbal abilities?

Creativity

When asked to name the most creative children in their classes, teachers consistently name more boys than girls, even though no significant differences between the sexes have been demonstrated from the results of tests of creative performance (Weitz, 1977). The real test, however, may not be comparative scores on creativity tests, but accomplishment in the real world. The inhibition on creativity may be the socialization process that channels men into potentially creative occupational fields and women away from creativity and into the wife and mother roles. In a related study (Forisha, 1976), male and female college students were compared on tests of creativity and then were assessed in terms of their creative production. There were no differences between the sexes in creative ability. However, men who scored highly on creative ability also scored highly on creative production. In other words, they did creative things and extended their creativity into the real world, whereas women with the same high abilities tended to be no more creatively productive than the less gifted students. The investigators concluded that women apparently have difficulty translating their creative inspirations into creative action. There is no basis for assuming that boys are born with a greater urge to transform the environment than girls or that boys are innately more creative than girls. Even though in peer-nomination studies, the number of men labeled "creative" far surpasses the number of women, both sexes have equal abilities, and it is apparently the socialization process that determines whether or not men and women will use their creativity productively.

Cognitive Style and Visual-Spatial Abilities

It is often said that women and men "think differently" and use different kinds of abilities or resources to demonstrate intelligence or reasoning. Gutmann (1970) has suggested that men are more "allocentric" or analytical and that they do not identify with a problem but seek to analyze and solve it. Women, on the other hand, are described as "autocentric," which means they can't separate themselves from their problems and can only learn through imitation of others. Others have suggested that women are more "global" in the way they perceive and solve problems, while men are again described as more "analytic." Broverman et al. (1968), in a controversial theory, claim that sex differences in cognitive or thinking abilities are based on the sex hormones estrogen, for women, and androgen, for men. They maintain that women are better at simple perceptual-motor tasks that require fast, accurate, repetitive responses, such as typing and color naming, while men are better at more complex tasks requiring restructuring or reorganization of the task and producing novel solutions. Freely translated, this means that "women are better at dicing celery and men are better at what we think of as thinking" (Tavris and Offir, 1977). Although Broverman et al. speak of each sex as "superior" in one kind of performance, the tasks are not regarded as equally important by society, and Broverman et al. ignore the superiority of women on linguistic tasks (Parlee, 1972).

The strongest evidence implying sex differences in thinking and spatial abilities comes from studies of field dependence-independence which involve the ability to separate distinctive features of figures from a competing background. Two of the best-known measures of this concept are the embedded-figures test and the rod-and-frame test. In an embedded-figures test you are required to find figures or items that are embedded or hidden within a larger picture. For example, a triangle may be embedded within a larger geometric design containing many other geometric figures such as squares, diamonds, rectangles, and circles, and you must separate the triangle from the rest of the design. In order to do this, you have to suppress your response to the whole drawing and concentrate on restructuring the parts of the design until you find the triangle. In the rod-and-frame test you sit in a darkened room and look at a projected outline of a rectangle or frame with a line or rod suspended inside of it. You are required to adjust the rod to a vertical position. In order to adjust the rod accurately you have to ignore the frame and concentrate on other cues such as the angle of your body relative to your chair and the floor. Sex differences on these field-dependent tasks do not emerge until adolescence, and then men begin and continue to score better than women throughout adulthood (Maccoby and Jacklin, 1974). Women tend to be more field-dependent and men more field-independent. On both of these tests, men are less distracted than women by misleading contextual cues.

The results of the research indicate that men and women do not differ on tests of analytic cognitive style unless the task specifically requires visual-spatial skills, and even then the sex-role appropriateness of the situation has been demonstrated to affect the performances of women and men. Naditch (1976), using the rod-and-frame test, told one group of men and women subjects that the test measured perceptual abilities related to intelligence and told another group of subjects that the test measured empathy. When they thought the test was measuring empathy, the women scored higher in field independence than the men, while men scored higher in field independence when they thought the test was measuring intelligence. Sherman (1974) has suggested that sex differences in visual-spatial ability may be based at least in part on differences in practice of sex-typed tasks. As we have noted previously, girls and boys are often given very different kinds of toys to play with starting at an early age. Boys are often given blocks and building materials, which develop spatial skills, while girls are often given dolls and sets of play dishes. Girls would be at a disadvantage in the field-dependence tests since their socialization has emphasized relating to others and being dependent upon them. Other investigations have suggested that male superiority on visual-spatial tasks is at least partially physiologically based and due to recessive genes or sex hormones (Waber, 1976; Petersen, 1976). In any case, our task is to assess the significance of such sex differences for real-life problems and choices.

Mathematical Ability

Mathematical ability, which is linked to visual-spatial ability, is extremely important since it is often the basis for entry into college and higher levels of education as well as a requirement for most scientific and technical fields. Tests measuring mathematical abilities, such as college aptitude tests, consistently show male superiority, and in the professional field of mathematics, men overwhelmingly outnumber women, especially when secondary schoolteachers are eliminated from the statistics (Weitz, 1977). Tobias (1976) maintains that sex differences in math ability are due to conditioned anxiety and cultural norms rather than to any inborn superiority in men. She states that women are especially likely to suffer from "mathophobia" and to avoid classes or fields of study that require mathematical ability or skills. Osen (1974) has used the term "the feminine mathique" to indicate the cultural values and beliefs that surround women and mathematics. Ability in mathematics is often considered "unfeminine," and as Osen points out, the popular stereotypes include the woman who is unable to balance the checkbook, as well as the empty-headed coed who is only interested in finding a husband for financial security.

Although men and women differ in specific areas of intellectual ability, most differences are small, average differences. Some of these differences may be biologically based, but none are of sufficient magnitude to limit the kinds of intellectual or social roles that men and women are capable of fulfilling (Kagan, 1975). Nevertheless, these small differences between the sexes are often interpreted as wide disparities, similar to those that have led to masculinity-femininity testing and to the establishing of separate sex norms and test biases, as we discussed in Chapter 3. Now we are ready to look at problems in intelligence or aptitude testing.

Intelligence Testing

Tests of general intelligence do not show differences in the average IQs of men and women, and this is not surprising, because the most widely used intelligence tests were designed to minimize sex differences. Items that differentiate between boys and girls or men and women have either been eliminated from these tests or the tests' authors have been careful to balance an item favoring men with an item favoring women. This doesn't mean that the test authors necessarily feel that men and women have equal abilities, however, but only that IQ tests have not been constructed to reflect these separate abilities. Wechsler, who developed the familiar and widely used Wechsler intelligence scales for adults and children, has maintained that women have different resources or degrees of abilities than men when "exercising whatever it is we call intelligence," and that men not only behave but "think differently" than women (Wechsler, 1958).

One issue in intelligence testing has been the validity of such testing and its meaning outside of the testing context. The selection of test items has been criticized as being culturally and sexually biased, and studies have been done in which items reflecting women's sex roles have been substituted for items reflecting men's roles in tests of mathematical abilities. For example, instead of designing math problems about rocket ships and race cars, problems describe situations that are considered to be of more relevance to women such as buying furniture or making clothes. When these types of items have been included in aptitude tests, performance for women has improved (Weitz, 1977). It seems that when women perceive a mismatch between the content of the item and their sex role, they perform below their capabilities.

Another criticism of intelligence testing concerns the relevance of test performance to performance in the real world. Even though aptitude scores often do correlate positively with school grade-point averages, school grades don't always accurately predict real-world performance. Examiner influences can also affect the performances of men and women on intelligence tests. In a study by Pedersen et al. (1975), subjects performed best under examiners of their own sex, and girls especially scored much higher when tested by women. The tests used were subtests of the Wechsler Intelligence Scale for Children which have been assumed to be relatively free of sex biases. The investigators concluded that the predominance of math teachers who are men and of English teachers who are women in our society may be producing an "educational artifact" in terms of sex-related aptitudes.

We have examined the relevant issues pertaining to sex differences in intelligence, and it now seems appropriate for us to consider the implications of these issues for our clients, students, and ourselves.

Implications for Service Providers

As service providers and as test takers yourselves, you have all had experiences with "intelligence" tests and "aptitude" tests. In both instances the results of the tests have been considered extremely important and may have affected your own lives as well as the lives of your students and your clients. As test takers, you have been accepted into college, graduate school, or professional school on the basis of these test scores and/or have been selected for employment positions or promotions. On the other hand, you may have been eliminated from consideration for a position or a field of study on the basis of your "aptitudes." If it hasn't happened to you, you can name friends and acquaintances who have had to change their life plans after doing poorly on these kinds of tests. As test users you are also in a potentially precarious and important position. You are often responsible for selecting intelligence tests and interpreting them, and the way you interpret the tests may have considerable effect, either positively or negatively, on the lives of your clients.

When you interpret intelligence-test scores it is important to keep in mind that the scores for most men and women overlap in the average range of intelligence, and when there are differences between the sexes, these are mean differences and usually small. For example, because women as a group tend to score higher on tests of verbal ability than men as a group doesn't mean that all women or even most women have higher verbal abilities than most men. Any individual man may outscore any individual woman and vice versa.

There is always a danger of overinterpreting or overgeneralizing from the results of these tests when making decisions for individual clients. For example, on the basis of test scores that indicate a tendency for higher visual-spatial and mathematical aptitudes for men, women have been excluded from consideration or guided away from careers in science, and, at the same time, their tendency toward lower scores on these abilities as a group has been used to explain the scarcity of women in the science professions. It can be a Catch-22 situation. Men and women are not *supposed* to do well in certain fields or professions, and if individual women or men *do* demonstrate aptitudes for a certain "inappropriate" sex-typed career or activity, they are still often excluded, and then the lack of men or women in that particular field is offered as "proof" that it is either exclusively "men's" work or "women's" work. Sex differences in ability aren't responsible for sex-typed career choices. Sex biases of society and test interpreters are responsible.

What can we as professionals and service providers do about this situation? Educators and guidance counselors can begin by encouraging both boys and girls to start thinking in terms of life plans and career potential from the time they enter school. The changes will be most significant for girls since they have not been traditionally socialized to prepare for careers as well as wife and mother roles. Boys can also benefit, however, from a perspective that allows them an even wider choice of opportunities including "women's" fields such as nursing or elementary school teaching as well as being a "househusband." Counselors need to be especially concerned about the failure of intelligent, creative girls to grow up to be intelligent, creative, and productive women. Parents can be taught and advised to provide, as nearly as possible, the same learning experiences for their sons and daughters including, for example, more emphasis on reading and creative writing for boys and more emphasis on building and creating *things* for girls. Mathematical ability is extremely important for both sexes since it is valued so highly by our technologically advanced society, and girls especially need to be helped to avoid "mathophobia." Girls aren't born with a built-in fear of math. They have to be taught that they are incompetent by parents, teachers, and counselors who buy the sex-role stereotypes. Similarly, boys aren't born with a fear of reading or learning foreign languages. Providing more role models for girls in mathematics and for boys in English will probably help, but first we need to change our sex-role requirements and awareness so that more men and women are encouraged to enter these professions to serve as role models. Changing the content of some test items, if they are clearly sex biased, may also be beneficial, but substituting one stereotype for another, for example, a man as an astronaut for a woman as a cook, will only reinforce sex-role stereotypes rather than change them. Better test content would include both men and women as astronauts and both men and women as cooks.

Aptitude is only one factor to be considered in career choice or employment potential and high "potential ability" does not necessarily mean high performance or achievement. Counselors, educators, employment managers, and other service providers need to keep in mind that additional factors such as motivation, socialization pressures, and achievement needs are often more accurate predictors of future performance than aptitude or intelligence. We will now focus our attention on these additional factors and examine their effects on women and men.

Achievement Motivation

The United States is an achievement-oriented society. When we ask children what they want to be when they grow up we are really asking them what they hope to achieve. Boys and girls from grade school through graduate school are required to take achievement tests, and many professionals are required to pass state licensing examinations before they can work in their chosen career field. The media emphasize striving, accomplishing, and success and persistently urge us to run faster, work harder, learn more, and to better ourselves and our life-styles.

Both men and women in our society value the importance of accomplishment and achievement, but women have not achieved equal prestige and status relative to men. Even though women constitute over 50 percent of the population in our society, most of them have not pursued life goals that require intellectual competence and leadership potential. Achievement behavior refers to the evaluation of performances against some standard of excellence, and although girls achieve at relatively high levels during childhood, their ultimate levels of achievement are considerably lower than those of men. The ratio of women to men underachievers increases with age until the college years and beyond when the women underachievers outnumber the men (Raph, Goldberg and Passow, 1966).

In a well-known study, Terman et al. (1947, 1959) began a longitudinal investigation of gifted boys and girls in 1921 and followed their life-progress into adulthood. When these gifted children grew up, almost half of the men became professionals in high-level occupations, and all of the eminent writers and artists from the original group were men. Only 11 percent of the gifted women were in professions and most of these women became teachers. Many of the women had married men who were high achievers, but the women did not achieve professionally themselves.

Even though a variety of explanations have been proposed to explain why women fail to strive for the goals inherent in the American dream of success, most of the early investigations of achievement motivation have focused on men. The most widely known theory of achievement motivation was proposed by McClelland et al. (1953). These early investigators assumed that achievement motivation consisted of learned tendencies that both energize and direct behavior toward specific goals. McClelland et al. developed an assessment technique using Murray's Thematic Apperception Test (TAT, 1938) which has been used extensively to investigate achievement motivation and has been correlated with achievement effort and academic and intellectual performance for men but not for women (Entwisle, 1972). McClelland et al. also assumed that more achievement motivation could be aroused in people by changing the conditions of the situation. For example, they believed that if people were told that their performance was related to intelligence and leadership qualities, their achievement motivation should increase. In studies with men these assumptions proved to be correct. With women, however, even though their basic levels of achievement motivation were approximately equal to those of men, the instructions assumed to enhance achievement motivation seemed to have little or no effect (Alper and Greenberger, 1967).

Atkinson and Feather (1966) maintained that two motives were essential for understanding achievement behavior: a hope for success and the fear of failure. For achievement motivation to be high, fear of failure should be less than hope for success. Men for whom hope of success is greater than fear of failure will set moderate levels of aspiration and demonstrate greatest achievement effort on moderately difficult tasks. If fear of failure dominates, however, men tend to set very low or very high levels of aspiration and show greatest achievement effort on easy or difficult tasks. Investigators have accumulated extensive data demonstrating relationships between achievement level, level of aspiration, task preference, and persistence for men, but during this progress, women have been virtually ignored (Weiner, 1972; Atkinson and Raynor, 1974).

Several more recent theories have been proposed to explain why men and women differ in their achievement behavior. At first it was assumed that girls and women are simply not as motivated to achieve as men. However, since boys and girls are fairly equal in achievement until adolescence, when performance for girls begins to decrease, we have to suspect that the different socialization process for the two sexes is responsible for these differences in behavior. Another explanation is that women and men are motivated by different needs and that for women, affiliation needs become more important than achievement needs. Therefore, while men strive to surpass some standard of excellence, women strive for social approval instead of achievement (Hoffman, 1972). However, even though women tend to score higher on scales that measure a desire for affiliation, there is little or no evidence to support the belief that women are more dependent upon social reinforcement than men (Maccoby and Jacklin, 1974). Furthermore, other investigators have argued that the achievement striving of men is more dependent upon the presence and approval of other people (Veroff et al., 1975; Kipnis, 1974). A third explanation for the differences between men and women is that although both sexes have similar needs for achievement, there are differences in the kinds of activities and goals that men and women use to meet these needs. In other words, men and women both strive to achieve, but they achieve in different ways. Social skills and interpersonal success are important for women as achievement goals, and men place higher value on other kinds of achievement such as academic endeavors and competitive sports. According to this explanation, it is only the *areas* of achievement that differ for women and men and not the *motives* for achievement (Deaux, 1976).

The notion of a unitary construct of achievement motivation may be too simplistic to account for the different patterns of behavior that men and women elect to express their achievement needs, according to Jackson, Ahmed, and Heapy (1976), who have hypothesized that there are several facets of achievement motivation. In a related study, Veroff et al. (1975) used three types of instruments to assess achievement motivation, including objective questions, projective questions, and behavioral assessment. The results of the analyses isolated six major factors: (1) assertive competence motivation (performing valued achievement in society), (2) task competence motivation, (3) fear of failure, (4) social comparison motivation (evaluating performance in terms of others), (5) future achievement orientation (long-term goals), and (6) hope of success. Women were found to be lower than men in assertiveness competence but were higher in hope of success. The investigators concluded that women are taught to value achievement only under certain conditions and in certain specific situations. They do not learn to value achievement in society above other goals, but they do learn to value task competence.

The Concept of Fear of Success

Atkinson and Feather first proposed the concepts of hope for success and fear of failure, and a few years later, Horner (1968) proposed another concept which she labeled fear of success. Horner maintains that many people, and especially women, have a motive to avoid success because they expect negative consequences if they are successful. According to Horner, these negative consequences include, for example, being socially rejected by other people. To find out whether or not men and women are afraid of success, Horner asked college students of both sexes to write a story about "John" or "Anne," a student at the top of his or her medical school class. The women students were always given the "Anne" story and the men the "John" story. Horner found that 65 percent of the women wrote stories that indicated that "Anne" was unhappy or had negative experiences as a result of her grades. For example, some stories suggested that "Anne" decided to quit medical school and become a nurse or that she became depressed and sick. On the other hand, only 10 percent of the men wrote stories that indicated unpleasant consequences for "John" as a result of success. Horner concluded that women as a group are more afraid of success than men.

Since Horner's original study, several other investigators have repeated her methods, and the results indicate that, depending upon the characteristics of the people writing the stories and upon the situations, the percentage of men and women who indicate fear of success may vary (Tressemer, 1974; Hoffman, 1974; and Zuckerman and Wheeler, 1975). There is some evidence that under certain conditions men indicate more fear of success than women. For example, when both men and women were asked to tell stories about both "Anne" and "John," both sexes told stories indicating fear of success when writing about "Anne" and men told even more fear-of-success stories (68 percent) than the women did (51 percent). In contrast, only 21 percent of the men and 30 percent of the women indicated negative consequences when referring to "John" in medical school. The investigators concluded that the stereotype is more powerful than the motive (Monahan et al., 1974).

Garkse (1975) also found the incidence of fear of success to be as high or higher for men than for women, and Horner herself (1972) reported an increase in the fear-of-success images expressed by men in response to cues depicting successful men. Katz (1973), on the other hand, found a significant decrease in the frequency of fear-of-success themes written by college women about "Anne" when the subjects were given additional information suggesting that the distribution of men and women in "Anne's" medical school class was approximately equal; in other words, that "Anne's" success was not inappropriate in terms of her sex role. Similarly, Alper (1973) obtained fewer fear-of-success stories from women when the reference to medical school was eliminated. The results of more recent research on fear of success do not support Horner's original hypothesis that women have more fear of success than men, but rather the results indicate that fear of success for both women and men depends upon the specific situational cues available and the sex of the person in the story. When Cherry and Deaux (1975) investigated fear of success for men and women in nontraditional settings, they found that while only 40 percent of the men indicated fear of success for "John" in medical school, 63 percent of the men anticipated negative consequences for "John" in nursing school. On the other hand, 50 percent of the women wrote fear-of-success stories for "Anne" in medical school, but only 13 percent described negative events for "Anne" in nursing school. The investigators concluded that when success occurs in a situation in which either women or men are not expected to achieve, both men and women will predict negative consequences for success. The sex and the situation must be considered together.

In her original investigation, Horner (1968) predicted that people who have high fear of success would perform more poorly in competitive situations than people who did not fear success. Makosky (1972) investigated this hypothesis and found that low fear-of-success women performed best on an anagram task when they were competing against a man or where the task had been labeled a "masculine" task by the investigator. On the other hand, women who had high fear of success performed better on the anagram task when competing against another woman or when the task was labeled "feminine." Makosky concluded that high fear of success does not mean that women are afraid to compete or try to achieve in every situation, but rather that they will only be afraid to compete when the task is "inappropriate" for their sex role or when their competitor is a man. In these situations the high fear-of-success women seem to anticipate negative consequences if they should succeed. Other investigations also have indicated that both men and women will avoid success if the consequences of that success appear to be unpleasant, but both sexes will also avoid failure when that outcome promises to be negative (Jellison et al., 1974; Fisher et al., 1974). It appears that neither men nor women fear success unless the consequences are explicit and negative. Depending upon the situation, they will approach the positive consequences and avoid the negative ones (Deaux, 1976).

Evaluation of Achievement

When women and men demonstrate competency and success, they are not always judged equally by other people. As we noted earlier in the Goldberg (1968) investigation, women rated identical articles to be of higher quality when they believed they were written by "John" instead of "Joan." In a related study, Deaux and Taynor (1973) had men and women college students evaluate other men and women as candidates for a scholarship program. Highly competent men were rated more positively than highly competent women by both sexes, and low-competence men were rated more negatively than low-competence women. The investigators concluded that there is a tendency for men and women to be rated unequally for equivalent performance. Similarly, Feather and Simon (1975) found that successful men and unsuccessful women were both evaluated more positively than unsuccessful men or successful women in a study concerning performance on qualifying examinations for several different occupations. Apparently, from the results of these investigations, there is a tendency for successful women and unsuccessful men to be judged negatively by other people in our society, since men are supposed to achieve and become successful and women are not supposed to be successful, at least not in "masculine" endeavors.

There are some situations, however, in which successful women may be evaluated as favorably or even more favorably for their performances than men. For example, Phetersen et al. (1971) discovered that one of the necessary ingredients appears to be the recognition by some authority of the performance in question. In other words, if some "expert" has already judged the woman's work positively, other people will also rate her achievement positively. When an identical painting was described alternately as painted by a man and as painted by a woman, both the man and the woman were judged to be identical in skill level *after* the painting had been declared a contest winner. Leventhal and Michaels (1971) suggested that people who perform well in spite of a handicap will be over-rewarded for their behavior. For example, a 5 ft. 2 in., thirty-year-old woman who runs a twenty-six-mile marathon race will be considered more deserving of credit than a 6 ft. 2 in., twenty-year-old man who runs the same distance in the same time. Taynor and Deaux (1973) found that women were seen as more deserving of a reward than men for the same behavior in a situation where a man was expected to perform successfully but a woman was not. When people were asked to rate the behavior of a woman or a man who successfully dealt with a situation involving a holdup man on an elevator, the woman's behavior was judged as superior to the man's behavior even though they had done the same things. There is also some support for the conclusion that women are judged positively for their achievement in a "masculine" field as long as they indicate that they also accept the sex roles of wife and mother (Shaffer and Wegley, 1974). On the other hand, men are not rated more positively by other people for succeeding in "feminine" occupations or for performing in ways that are unexpected for their sex roles (Deaux, 1976).

Attributing Cause for Performance

Not only are the successes and failures of women and men judged differently by people within our society, but also the causes of achievement behavior are perceived as different for the two sexes. According to Heider (1958), who first developed the theory of attribution, people can use internal, or personal, explanations to describe success or failure or they can use external, or situational, explanations. For example, an internal explanation might be based on the aptitude or ability of the individual, while an external explanation might be based on luck or the difficulty of the task. In part, our choice of explanations depends upon our prior experience with the person or task involved. If a friend of yours is an excellent tennis player and wins a championship match, you would probably attribute your friend's success to ability. But if your friend loses the match, you would probably attribute the loss to bad luck, poor playing conditions, or an extremely competent opponent.

The sex of the performer also seems to be important. When both men and women are successful on the same or similar tasks, other people attribute the performances of the men to skill or ability but attribute the performances of the women to luck (Deaux and Emswiller, 1974). In situations where luck is not considered to be a plausible explanation, such as in a study by Feldman-Summers and Kiesler (1974) where subjects were required to attribute causes for the success of either Dr. Mark Greer or Dr. Marcia Greer, the explanations still tend to differ as a function of sex. Luck was not often cited to explain the success of either "Mark" or "Marcia," but the male subjects, especially, attributed more ability to "Mark" and indicated that "Marcia" had tried harder and had an easier task. In contrast, the female subjects agreed that "Marcia" had tried harder, but they felt her task had been more difficult.

In studies where failure conditions were described, the woman's failure was explained by a lack of ability and hard work, whereas the man's failure was attributed to bad luck or unfair conditions. In other words, when women succeed, it is because they are lucky or try harder, but they are not seen as having the same degree of ability as men, and when women fail it's because of their own inability. Men, on the other hand, are seen as more capable than women, and when they succeed it's because of their abilities. When they fail, however, external explanations are given such as bad luck or task difficulty (Deaux, 1976).

Expectancy and Self-Evaluations

When men and women rate themselves, there are no differences between the sexes in degree of self-esteem, even though their basis for self-esteem may be different. At the same time, however, there are consistent differences between men and women in specific areas that require self-confidence (Deaux, 1976). On tasks covering a wide range of behavior and in a variety of situations, men consistently predict that they will perform better than women and feel that they have performed better than women, even though in the majority of the situations men and women do equally well. Women, on the other hand, tend to underestimate their future performance and to feel they have done worse than men even when they have performed equally well (Crandall, 1969; Feather, 1969). When college students were asked to estimate their grades for the next semester, the men predicted they would do as well or better, while women thought they would not do as well as they had in the past. Actual grades for the next semester showed no differences between the men and the women, and although both sexes had predicted inaccurately, men had made the greatest number of errors. Furthermore, when cues were given to the students that indicated that they were either capable or not capable, the women tended to focus on the negative aspects of the cues and the men on the positive aspects (Crandall, 1975).

Stake (1976) found that both men and women set higher goals for their own performance when they are told that members of their own sex typically outperformed those of the other sex, and Deaux and Farris (1974) found that women expected to do less well than men when they were told that men typically do better on a certain task than women. Apparently men's and women's estimates of success are influenced not only by the difficulty of the task, but also by whether they think the task is appropriate for their sex role. Providing women, especially, with information that contradicts the norm may be an effective way to raise the levels of the goals they establish for themselves.

Men and women also explain their own behavior differently. Men who are successful tend to attribute their success to ability and effort, whereas women attribute their success to task ease or chance. When men fail, they attribute their failure to bad luck or task difficulty, whereas women tend to attribute failure to their own lack of ability to do well. In other words, women are reluctant to take credit for success, but they are more willing than men to blame themselves for failure. Even though women may be more "realistic" than men when confronted with failure, the consequences of their willingness to accept personal blame can be detrimental for future performance (Deaux, 1976). A man or a woman who attributes success to a stable internal factor such as ability is likely to feel that successful outcomes are under his or her control and will approach a new achievement situation with confidence. Attributing failure to unstable external factors such as bad luck is also unlikely to inhibit future achievement behavior. On the other hand, the man or woman who attributes success to external factors such as luck or task ease and failure to internal ones such as lack of ability may feel reluctant to strive for success in new situations. Deaux et al. (1975) gave college students the opportunity to play a game of skill or a game of chance. Approximately 75 percent of the men chose the game of skill, while 65 percent of the women chose the game of chance. Although both men and women indicated that it was more important to succeed in the game of skill, the estimates given by the women for their own probability of success on the skill game were much lower than the estimates given by the men. The authors concluded that the preferences expressed by the women for the game of chance were related to their expectancy for success. Women approach a task with lower expectations for their performance than men.

We have now compared the behavior of women and men on several different aspects of achievement and achievement motivation. Let us now turn our attention to a discussion of the implications of these different aspects of achievement behavior for our own work with women and men.

Implications for Client Services

You should now be aware of the difficulties inherent in evaluating the meaning of sex differences in achievement. Both men and women indicate that they value accomplishment, and both sexes feel that success in academic-vocational areas is the most prestigious and important type of achievement behavior for our society. While most men strive for this definition of achievement, most women do not. We know that girls and women are as motivated to achieve as are boys and men, and until adolescence, girls achieve academically and competitively and often outperform boys in many achievement-oriented activities. During adolescence, however, boys begin to achieve more and girls begin to achieve less, at least in terms of achievement defined as academic-vocational success.

What can we, as mental-health professionals, do about this situation? We could support the status quo and continue to counsel boys and men to behave "appropriately" by achieving academically and vocationally and to counsel girls and women to behave "appropriately" by vicariously enjoying the academic and vocational achievement of their husbands and sons. If we do this, however, we will have to ignore the changing social scene and we will soon become obsolete. On the other hand, we could change our definition of achievement for women and focus more on interpersonal skills and levels of success for marriage, childrearing, and related skills. With two separate definitions of achievement, one for women and one for men, both sexes could be assessed on achievement measures according to their "appropriate" skills. We already have some evidence to indicate that this approach results in higher correlations between motivation and performance for women. For example, Friedrich (1976) expanded the projective measures of achievement motivation to include achievement in social skills and other areas related to the experiences of most women, and she found, as expected, that achievement-motivation scores for women correlated higher with performance using these types of measures. Also, these two definitions of achievement would more closely reflect the current norms of our society. How do you as a mental-health professional feel about this type of approach to measuring achievement and achievement motivation? Think about it. It sounds relatively logical and reasonable, and other social scientists have already suggested and endorsed this method. If you are a man, it really doesn't change much for you personally, or does it? If you're a woman, you are already achieving according to the "masculine" definition of achievement and success, and you may have even stronger feelings about this suggestion for separate definitions of achievement. If we move in this direction, aren't we still endorsing the status quo? More women will obtain high achievement scores, but they will still be achieving in areas that do not have leadership potential or status within our society. Even if we change existing achievement measures to include areas of social skills and related tasks and we obtain high scores for both sexes on these same measures, we will have accomplished what the general IQ tests have accomplished in that we will have covered up the differences between the sexes without changing them.

What other approaches might we try? We have discussed previously some of the ways that we as educators, counselors, therapists, and parents might attempt to influence and change the socialization process for boys and girls. By becoming aware of the sex-role issues ourselves and communicating our knowledge to our students, our colleagues, and our individual clients, we may be able to bring about at least some small but significant changes. Since both men and women tend to increase their achievement-striving behavior when they have been given information that indicates that their behavior is appropriate for their sex roles, we can provide that information whenever possible, or we can provide role models and career information that contradict the stereotyped norms, especially for women. We can be aware that socialization pressure is extremely heavy on men who aren't successful according to the standard definition of achievement as well as on women who are, and we can attempt to help these men as well as these women to achieve in ways that are best for them individually.

We have examined the ways that men and women evaluate themselves and others and the ways that the two sexes attribute causes for successful and unsuccessful performance. In the next chapter we will look at the effects of these behavior patterns on career choice and career counseling.

5

Career Choice and Career Counseling

Career Development

American women and men do not achieve or contribute equally to our society when achievement is defined in terms of educational and career productivity. Men and women are equally intelligent and believe equally in the importance of career achievement, but women do not achieve as much success and prestige through productive work as men, even though women as a group make up over 50 percent of our population and over 40 percent of our labor force (Women's Bureau, 1976).

The life plans of men are usually shaped by their career goals, especially for men who aspire to professional careers, and we commonly identify men in terms of their work and their occupations. Men are expected to be task-oriented, competitive, and productive and often are expected to place a secondary value on their other life roles, such as husband and father. Early in their lives, emphasis is placed on achievement and competition, sometimes at the expense of emotional growth, and often with the result of a rising incidence of stress-related diseases, such as ulcers and heart attacks, that can lead to early deaths (Fasteau, 1974).

For women, on the other hand, whatever they may achieve in the world of work, their primary identity in society is social. Even single women are more often defined by their marital status than single men, and men, regardless of their involvement with their families, are defined by their work roles (Weitz, 1977). When men do survive until retirement age, they are often at a loss as to how to find a sense of meaning for the rest of their lives. For women, however, the sense of meaninglessness or dissatisfaction in life may occur at an earlier age. Alper (1974) refers to the illusive quality of achievement motivation in women and the ambivalence created by their desires for both achievement and affiliation with men and their fears that success in one area may rule out success in the other. In order to resolve this ambivalence, many women try to find indirect achievement satisfaction through the successes of important men in their lives (Lipman-Blumen and Leavitt, 1976). While vicarious achievement may meet the needs of some women, others, especially those who are intelligent and have high levels of achievement motivation, are often frustrated and resentful because of their own lack of productive achievement experiences. For this reason, as well as for other reasons as we will soon discuss, the sex roles, especially for women, are shifting and women are participating in increasing numbers in our labor force. At every stage in the life cycle, women are more likely now than in previous years to be employed (Hoffman, 1977). At the same time, however, our socialization patterns still reflect stereotyped role expectations for men and women, and the corresponding changes expected in work and social roles for men seem to be slow in developing.

Theories of Career Development

Because women have not been traditionally expected to include careers as a part of their life plans, almost all theories of career development are theories about men. Osipow (1968) in his book reviewing the theories of career development indicates that the theories are "masculine-based" and that only a few concepts or explanations have been developed to deal with the special problems and experiences in the career development of women. For example, Super (1957, 1972) maintains that career development can best be understood by examining the process from a life-style perspective. According to Super, people follow specific patterns and strive to implement their self-concepts by choosing careers that are most likely to permit them self-expression. He defines four types of possible career patterns for men, including "stable," "conventional," "unstable," and "multiple-trial." Super has suggested additional career patterns for women, including "stable homemaking," "interrupted" (leaving work to become homemakers and then returning to work later), and "double-tract" (marrying but continuing to work). He also defines the "conventional" pattern differently for men and women. For women, "conventional" is interpreted as working after education but not after marriage. It is interesting to note that there are no "homemaking" or "interrupted" patterns as possibilities for men, and even though most men fit Super's "double-tract" pattern (career plus marriage) they are not included in this category (Harmon, 1977).

Maslow (1970) has theorized that people function according to specific needs. These include physiological needs such as hunger or thirst at the lowest level and then progress, in order, to needs for safety, needs for love, needs for esteem, and, finally, to the highest level of needs, the needs for self-actualization or self-fulfillment. According to Maslow, we do not become aware of our higher-order needs for esteem and self-fulfillment until the lower-order needs are satisfied. For example, people who are afraid for their safety or who are worried about having a place to sleep or a meal to eat will not be thinking about fulfilling their achievement potential in an appropriate career. It is only after our lower-order needs are taken care of that we are motivated and ready to deal with the higher-order needs. Men have traditionally satisfied their own physiological and safety needs through work which produces money to buy food and shelter, and they have been able to satisfy most of their needs for love by being able to support and protect their wives and families. For their efforts, they have traditionally been rewarded by the esteem of others in society and by having the self-satisfaction of fulfilling their appropriate sex-role requirements. Even men who work in comparatively low-status jobs, such as repetitive assembly-line work, are applauded by society for supporting themselves and their families, and they have the self-esteem that accompanies productive achievement, even if it doesn't allow for gratification of the highest-order needs of self-actualization or self-expression.

The situation is very different for women, however. They have not traditionally fulfilled their own lower-order needs, but have relied on the men in their lives to provide them with food and safety. In return, women have maintained the home and raised the children and have been rewarded by having their needs for love and belonging fulfilled. At the same time, however, they have not had as much opportunity to fulfill their higher-order needs as have men. The woman who leaves the home to provide for her own physiological and safety needs may be in the position of risking the loss of the sense of belonging and love and esteem she receives for fulfilling the traditional female sex role. While men are loved and esteemed more as they become successful, as we noted in the last chapter, women are not always praised for their successes, especially in "masculine" careers. A woman may have to compromise her need for self-esteem in order to receive esteem from others, and for women more than men, there is often a conflict between these higher-order needs (Harmon, 1977). Since esteem is necessary before self-actualization can be attained, most women in our society have less hope than men for self-expression and self-fulfillment.

Holland (1966) has theorized that there are six possible types of people, including "realistic," "intellectual," "social," "conventional," "enterprising," and "artistic," and six corresponding work environments. According to Holland, most people can be categorized as one of these six types. However, almost all of the research based upon his theory has been conducted with men as subjects. Holland did later develop a classification scheme for women which includes four classes of social behavior as well as the intellectual, conventional, and artistic categories (Holland and Whitney, 1968), but few studies have investigated this classification scheme. For a more thorough review of the masculine-based theories of career development, refer to Osipow, 1968.

Career Development for Women

A few theories have been developed specifically to deal with career development for women. Psathas (1968) has described several factors which appear to influence whether or not a woman will pursue a career. He maintains that for women, as for men, there is a strong relationship between occupational role and sex role and that the types of factors that are most influential for women include the age at which the woman marries (if she decides to marry), her husband's economic situation, and her husband's attitudes about her working. Zytowski (1969) theorized that there are distinctive differences in the work lives of women and men. According to Zytowski, the developmental stages are different for the two sexes, and their patterns of career participation differ. He further stated that although the current model role for women is that of homemaker, ultimately women's and men's roles will be similar. Zytowski also maintained that vocational and homemaker participations were mutually exclusive, a theory that appears to have been refuted by the evidence that at least 40 percent of all married women are employed (Women's Bureau, 1971). Wolfson (1972) found that career patterns were not predictable from information gathered about college freshmen women, but that career patterns could be predicted from information collected five years later. Variables related to levels of education and marriage were the most significant predictors of career patterns for women.

Bernard (1973) maintains that there are several patterns that women can follow in order to arrange the four major factors (marriage, children, education, and a profession) in their lives. She feels that the worst possible pattern in terms of establishing a successful career is the one in which the woman leaves her work for marriage or has children before completing her education and beginning to work. According to Bernard, such a break interrupts the woman's career at a time when her career plans are least stable, and a lengthy interruption also creates family dependence upon her which in the long run makes it more difficult for her to resume her career plans. Although this is the current career pattern for almost half of all young American women, it is the most damaging pattern because the most creative periods in the lives of both men and women are often the very years the women are encouraged to stay home and raise a family. Furthermore, when these women return to the labor force they typically become assistants and technicians rather than leading professionals in their career fields. On the other hand, the woman who chooses not to drop out may also choose not to get married or at least not to have children. The choice is often "either/or," a choice not faced by men. If a woman chooses to attempt both a career and a family, she is likely to discover that she needs to be a "wonderwoman" to handle the dual responsibilities effectively. Except in the cases of the most energetic and exceptional women, these responsibilities can be another barrier to achievement in higher-level career positions (O'Leary, 1974).

Scanzoni (1975) has developed a model of career development for women that includes considerable changes in the nature of the family and of the participation of women in the work force. According to Scanzoni, the pattern begins with full-time premarital employment which is influenced positively by education. Employment, education, and "sex-role modernity" combine to postpone marriage and increase the likelihood that the woman will work full-time after marriage. These factors have also been shown to increase the interval between marriage and the first child and reduce the number of children born. The age of marriage, especially for women, has increased and so has the tendency for women to live on their own before marriage. Such experiences and opportunities for independent living and work experiences will have an impact on the life plans of women with regard to their marriages and their careers. Weitzman (1975) points out that although high-achieving women who have careers—for example, doctors, lawyers, professors, or corporate executives—are often referred to as deviants from the norm, these are the women who have broken from the traditional mold and are formulating their own model for career development for women. She maintains that there must be a systematic study of the socialization of high-achieving women to discover what factors in the socialization process were different for these women than for women in general. In the next section we will look at some of the factors that influence career development and career choice for both men and women.

Factors Affecting Career Development and Career Choice

For most men in American society, there is no question whether they will work. They are expected to achieve and to work productively as part of their stereotyped sex role. For most women, on the other hand, our society does not dictate the decision, but rather the woman herself must decide whether to include a career as part of her life plan. There are two major explanations often given to account for these differences in sex-role requirements. The first is that men are biologically more aggressive than women and therefore better suited for achievement and competitive productivity. Since a predisposition for aggression has been demonstrated to be related to biological factors in boys and men (Maccoby and Jacklin, 1974), this explanation seems to suggest that the masculine role of worker and provider is inevitable. In our modern society, however, while being assertive often helps both men and women achieve their goals, being forcefully aggressive and dominating others by the threat of violent aggressive behavior is usually not necessary. Also, our society does not really value overt aggression in either sex, and as we noted in Chapter 1, parents try to discourage aggression in both their sons and their daughters. Therefore, the explanation that men are naturally more aggressive than women fails to account for the major differences in the life plans of the two sexes. The other major explanation is based upon the different socialization processes for women and men that require men to become workers and women to become wives and mothers. There are several important factors in the socialization process that apparently influence both women and men and can determine how career development and career choice occur for both sexes.

Parents and Family

Various family situations have been demonstrated to encourage or discourage occupational aspirations for boys and girls, and the roles of the parents appear to be especially important. Achievement behavior is positively related to various forms of parental encouragement, including positive reinforcement, attempts at acceleration (for example, placing excessive importance on the child's level of achievement), and criticism for lack of effort (Stein and Bailey,

1973). In a related study, Hermans et al. (1972) found that positive reinforcement from the parents was associated with high achievement motivation, whereas withholding reinforcement after success was related to test anxiety in their children. Also, Spence et al. (1978) have concluded that high levels of competitiveness and work mastery for high school and college men are found most frequently in traditional (masculine father-feminine mother) families and least frequently in undifferentiated (low masculine and low feminine) families and in masculine father-undifferentiated mother families. For women, Spence et al. discovered that high work mastery was found most often in families with an androgynous (high masculine and high feminine) father and least often in families with an undifferentiated mother.

The role of the mother is apparently extremely important. The attitudes that the mothers hold about employment are especially significant for girls, and if the mother is herself employed, her employment apparently affects the career attitudes and behavior of both her sons and her daughters (Hoffman, 1977). For example, one effect of maternal employment is that the division of tasks within the house is sometimes affected. In these families, not only do children have as a role model a woman who works outside of the home, but they also see their fathers helping more with the housework. The mother still maintains the largest share of the household duties, but the children see the father taking on some of the tasks, such as washing the dishes or running the vacuum, that have been conventionally defined as part of the "feminine" sex role (Hoffman and Nye, 1974). In related studies, sons and daughters of working mothers were found to be less stereotyped in their perceptions of men and women and to see women as less restricted to their homes and more active in the world and fathers as warmer and more affectionate. Daughters of working mothers describe women as more competent and effective than do daughters of nonworking mothers, and sons of working mothers see men as warmer and more expressive than do sons of nonworking mothers (Baruch, 1972; Miller,

1975). Hoffman and Nye (1974) also found that college women who are career-oriented or are planning less conventionally "feminine" careers are likely to be daughters of working mothers, and there is some evidence that the daughters of working mothers are more independent and autonomous than daughters of nonworking mothers. Weitz (1977) points out that we should not overlook the influence of mothers in the traditional role of housewife as potentially *negative* role models for their daughters, especially if they are obviously unhappy because of their lack of careers. In some cases, the daughters of these unhappy women will decide upon a career in order to avoid the limited roles in which they see their own mothers.

The role of the father is apparently equally as important as the role of the mother in fostering achievement motivation in his children, and some research has indicated that the father may be an even more important influence than the mother (Block et al., 1974). As we have already noted, fathers typically participate more in the home when the mother is employed, and there is some evidence that indicates that the father's increased participation in childrearing facilitates the development of independence and achievement in both girls and boys (Hoffman, 1977). As we noted in Chapter 1, there is also evidence that fathers, to a greater degree than mothers, tend to treat their sons and daughters differently and to reinforce the existing sex-role stereotypes. However, it has been found that husbands of working wives are less traditional than husbands of women who are unemployed (Hoffman and Nye, 1974). Apparently, men become more aware of sex biases in conventional stereotyped roles when they are directly affected by the consequences of these sex biases; for example, when their wives earn less money because they are women or are refused promotions or employment positions because employers feel they should be home taking care of their children.

Hennig and Jardin (1977) investigated the relationships between high-achieving women and their fathers and concluded that these women have had a close relationship with their fathers, often because there was not a brother in the family who competed with them for the father's attention. Many of these women described their fathers as supportive and encouraging them to achieve. Weitzman (1975) speculates that an especially strong stimulus for achievement motivation in women is a strong father-daughter relationship in which the father makes his love and approval dependent upon her performance rather than showing unconditional support whether or not his daughter achieves. A father who considers his daughter's achievement as crucial to her success in life can motivate his daughter to "masculine" achievement. As Weitzman further notes, this father-daughter relationship has a parallel in research on achievement motivation for men in which McClelland (1964) has demonstrated that a strong mother-son relationship, in which the mother makes her love conditional on her son's success, is most conducive to fostering achievement motivation in men.

Baumrind (1972) maintains that there are two patterns of parental authority which facilitate competence in children: the "authoritative" parent who exercises firm control and sets limits but values independence and individuality, and the "harmonious" parent who has control but does not exercise it because the children seem to know what behavior is expected of them. According to Baumrind, with these types of parents the child's personhood is respected and valued, and competent achievement behavior is not only encouraged but expected. Girls and boys do not need different kinds of preparation in order to develop skills and abilities, but more conscious effort may be required in order to foster these results in girls, since prevailing social pressures may not support achievement behavior in women. Baumrind further suggests that girls as well as boys should be taught to compete in sports and other contests and taught to win and lose gracefully as well as to become assertive and to defend their rights as individuals. Rubovits (1975) also maintains that within the same families, girls and boys should receive the same social-learning experiences so that when women as well as men are faced with the necessity to work they will be prepared for the competitive marketplace and be able to choose work that is realistic for their potential.

Role Models and Reference Groups

Role models outside of the family can also influence career development and career choice. We have already discussed the importance of teachers and guidance counselors and have mentioned the importance of college professors, practicum supervisors, and employers in the socialization process for men and women. Weitz (1977) has noted that male and female college professors may influence the career decisions of their students at a critical period in the career-development process. She maintains, however, that this influence may "backfire" for women students since many female college professors beyond middle age have never married and may present negative role models for aspiring female professors. On the other hand, she points out that the older, unmarried female faculty members really do not present an accurate role model, since currently, most younger academic women marry. Bernard (1964) has noted that even university professors have different sex-related career values and that female professors are more likely to show concern for developing students and promoting scholarship, and to be active in providing service to the university, whereas men are usually more concerned with career prestige and academic power.

Reference groups and peer groups can also influence the career development of both women and men. When intelligent boys and girls are placed together in honors classes or even in special schools, such as the Bronx High School of Science in New York or New Trier High School in Chicago, the levels of peer-group aspiration and faculty encouragement tend to be higher than for other groups of adolescents. Settings such as these may be particularly important in encouraging career choices, especially for women, because the resulting peer-group contacts are likely to reinforce achievement rather than to discourage this behavior (Weitz, 1977). Once men and women have entered their chosen career fields they tend to compare themselves to others in the same fields and to measure their progress according to this established reference group.

Darley (1976) maintains that because the role requirements of having a career and being a good husband and father are not contradictory and because most husbands and fathers have careers, men can evaluate their occupational and sex-role performances fairly easily and reliably. Women with careers, on the other hand, have a more difficult time finding relevant reference groups since most of their colleagues are likely to be men. Of the few colleagues who are women, some will be single, others will be married, and some will have children, but they are still likely to differ from each other in these important ways. The career woman who is also married and who may or may not have children will often find herself being evaluated for her performance in her wife and mother roles by other women who do not have careers and do not understand the dual role demands. According to Darley, a woman who tries to combine wife and mother roles with a career is caught between two reference groups which often have conflicting values and standards for evaluating her performance, and she will also have difficulty evaluating her own performance in her career and sex roles.

We have discussed some of the ways that fathers' attitudes can affect the career choices of their children. For women especially, the attitudes of other significant men in their lives, such as their husbands, boyfriends, professors, and employers, can determine whether or not they pursue a career or even which career they will choose. Entwisle and Greenberger (1970) found that both sexes responded negatively when they were asked whether women should work in a "masculine" occupation. The greatest difference of opinion for boys and girls occurred when they were asked whether women should work at all, with most of the girls responding "yes" and most of the boys responding "no." When high school students were asked the same question (Nelson and Goldman, 1969), most of the men indicated acceptance of the employment role for women except in the case of their own wives, and when college men were asked their opinions about employment for women (McMillin, 1972), nearly half of the men would not consider the possibility of a lifetime career for their wives, even with an interruption for child-raising. For these college students there were differences in opinions found according to the career areas that the men were themselves pursuing. For example, men who were majoring in science, business, and mathematics preferred less career involvement for women than men who were majoring in education or the social sciences. Kaley (1971) investigated the attitudes of married professional men and women and found that while the professionally employed women have positive attitudes toward a combination of career and family roles for women, professional men have negative attitudes about the dual role and feel that even qualified women should be discouraged from seeking higher education and professional careers.

Other Factors that Influence Career Development and Career Choice

Other factors that have been found to influence career development and career choice for both women and men include social class, region of the country, and "demographic pressures" (Weitz, 1977). Educational and career levels are directly related to social class, with the most stress on higher education and professional careers stemming from the middle- and upper-class value systems. The region of the country in which one lives can also influence career development, especially for women, and there is some evidence that southern women, for example, are less likely than northeastern, midwestern, or far western women to pursue careers such as medicine. According to Weitz, "demographic pressures" means a "shortage of men," such as that which occurred in America during World War II, when women were encouraged to attend medical and professional schools and to work outside of the home in war-related occupations.

Hunt and Hunt (1977) have theorized that another factor affecting career development and choice is family support, particularly husband or wife support. According to the Hunts, people who are most successful in professional careers tend to have supportive services provided by their wives or husbands which are often essential for top-level career performance. For example, the wife maintains the home, essentially raises the children, and provides other services for her husband so that he is free from the responsibilities of day-to-day family life and can concentrate on his career. The advantages of this "two-person career" are obvious for the husband, who is able to assume a public productive role without forfeiting his husband or father roles.

The reverse pattern—the husband remaining at home and supporting his wife's career—is quite rare, but there are a few families where this pattern does occur. When the woman works, however, the pattern is more likely to be either the "dual-worker" pattern where one spouse has a "career" and the other has a "job," or the "dual-career" pattern where both have careers and at the same time attempt to maintain a family life. The Hunts maintain that the dual-career pattern is the most difficult for both the husband and the wife since neither has a supportive spouse at home who is handling the child care and the domestic chores. The consequences of the dual-career pattern often include either one spouse withdrawing to facilitate the career of the other or the couple separating to pursue careers without the problems of having to coordinate two separate schedules and finding career opportunities in the same geographic locations.

These investigators compare each member of the dual-career pattern to the single professional man who is sometimes handicapped by the absence of a wife as a social asset as well as a supportive helper, and they feel that both husbands and wives need many supportive services provided for them if they are going to become especially successful in their careers. In our society, it is almost always the women who limit their own career aspirations to enable their husbands to pursue their careers, because most women cannot fully delegate their family responsibilities to others. According to the Hunts, even single career women would be able to achieve more and rise more easily to the top of their professions if they had a "wife" at home to take care of day-to-day responsibilities for them.

Since it appears to be more difficult for women to develop careers without interruptions and more difficult for them to choose careers or jobs that are appropriate for their potential, why do so many women in our society work?

Why Women Work

Tavris and Offir (1977) maintain that there are three main reasons why more and more American women are working: economic conditions, educational opportunities, and declining family size. Women work because they need the money the same as men. Furthermore, many more women are completing college than ever before and are going on to enter professional schools and Ph.D. programs. For example, in 1960, only 6 percent of the students in medical schools were women, while in 1974, 18 percent of all medical students were women (U.S. Department of Labor, 1974). Finally, women are having fewer children; in 1974 the birthrate in the United States hit an all-time low for this century with an average 1.9 children per family (Glick, 1975) and, as a result, women have more time available to work since fewer years are spent in child care and related activities. Life expectancy for women has increased to seventy-four years, and since most women have given birth to their last child by age thirty, they can expect approximately forty years of adult life that will not be occupied by the care of small children (Forisha, 1978). Also, Spence et al. (1978) have pointed out that being widowed at a relatively young age is a realistic possibility and that divorce is becoming more common and socially acceptable. The vast majority of divorced and widowed women in our society have limited financial resources and are usually expected to work to support themselves, since alimony is less certain, and they may also have minor children to support.

Hoffman (1974) maintains that working women feel more competent than nonworking women and hold less conventional views of sex roles, even though it is not clear whether these factors are the causes or the effects of their working status. According to Hoffman, women work because of their desire to benefit society as well as their need for social contact. Also, a paycheck is tangible evidence of the value of a woman's skills and gives her the status and satisfaction of achieving on her own. Women are most likely to be working if they are young, single, educated, and black; but mothers without husbands, wives who have husbands with low incomes, women with no preschool children, and women who live in areas where jobs are available are also likely to be working (Hoffman, 1977). An interesting finding by Astin (1973) is that women who pursue careers often show an exceptional aptitude for mathematics, and mathematics skills are often the best predictors of career productivity for women.

Career Behavior

Once men and women have made career choices and entered the work world, they are often treated quite differently by their employers and their coworkers, and their own behavior often reflects their sex roles. For example, employers sometimes explain that women aren't promoted as quickly or as often as men because women are happy where they are. In a study by Crowley et al. (1973), 64 percent of the working men and only 48 percent of the working women said they wanted to be promoted. More women than men said that having friendly coworkers was very important, and they attached more importance to the job surroundings, the time it took to commute, and the hours they worked. Kanter (1976a), however, also observed that men and women often have different *opportunities* for promotion and that the low desire for promotion among women is related to expectancy for promotion. Both women and men who are trained professionals and have high-ranking jobs expect to be promoted and their achievement ambitions are similar. At the same time, both men and women who are in "dead-end" jobs such as factory workers, secretaries, or clerks, often realize that there are little or no opportunities for advancement, and they then feel less attached to their jobs, fantasize about leaving, and tend to emphasize family life over work. The kind of a job a person has often determines whether he or she enjoys working; and when a person dislikes work, he or she usually cares more about the job conditions than the demands of the work itself.

Tokens

Kanter also maintains that stereotyped sex-role behavior is almost always demonstrated by women and men who serve "token" roles in their occupations. For example, the only woman who works in a large corporation or in a university is a "token" and is isolated from others of her sex. Similarly, a male nurse is often a "token" worker in an occupation represented almost exclusively by women. The problem with being a token, according to Kanter, is that coworkers tend to see the token worker as unique rather than as a person similar to others of his or her sex. Furthermore, the coworker group not only sees the token in a stereotyped way, but also pressures the token to behave in a stereotyped way.

Kanter (1976b) has identified some of the ways a token woman worker must behave if she wants to be accepted by her coworkers. She can play the mother, who comforts the men and bakes cookies and makes coffee; the sex object, who entices the men to compete for her; or the kid sister, who plays the office pet and adds humor without threat. If she does not play one of these acceptable roles, however, she may be treated with hostility and be referred to as "the bitch." All tokens face the same predicament; that is, how to become less visible and more accepted by the group. Some people fulfill the stereotype expected of them, while others try to be as inconspicuous as possible. Concealing achievement and temporarily reducing effort are other ways of coping with possible conflicts (Stein and Bailey, 1973).

Some women develop the "Queen Bee" syndrome. According to Tavris and Offir (1977), Queen Bees are rare women who reach the top levels of a "masculine" occupation. They have no use for other women and like the rewards they receive for being "special." For example, as the only woman, the Queen Bee is highly praised as a remarkable exception to her sex, and there is no way she is going to suggest that she is not so special or that other women might also be well qualified and capable. Queen Bees don't want competition any more than men do, and they don't see why other women should be given any special considerations because of their sex. Besides, they have worked hard to achieve success and it's fun to be the only woman at the top.

Barriers and Discrimination

Men and women, but especially women, can encounter other career barriers that thwart achievement, and as we noted in the case of the Queen Bee, women as well as men are responsible for these external barriers. Women have been discriminated against in admission to graduate and professional schools and in obtaining jobs, particularly high-status ones. Even though Astin (1969) found that over 90 percent of women with Ph.D.'s were employed eight years later and were serious, productive professionals, Ekstrom (1972) discovered that women were still being refused admission to "inappropriate" graduate programs and quotas were being set on women's acceptance in other fields, whereas men were being accepted with lower qualifications. Sex biases favoring men have also been found in the granting of scholarships, grants, and assistantships, but women have been able to obtain more money in loans than men. As we have previously discussed and as Ekstrom's findings support, many high school and college counselors of both sexes hold sex-role biases and try to discourage women and men from entering "inappropriate" career fields. Similarly, family and societal pressures may also influence a man or a woman to give up an "inappropriate" career and to switch to a more "appropriate" one. In a well-known study, Fidell (1970) sent out fake applications for career positions in psychology departments in various universities. The biographies and references were identical, but some were for "Patrick" and others were for "Patricia." The responses from the various universities indicated that "Patrick" was offered more appointments and appointments of higher rank (associate or full professor rather than assistant professor). Full professorships, the highest rank, were only offered to "Patrick." In other studies, differences were found in the evaluations for men and women once they were hired for teaching positions (Siskel, 1976; Kaschak, 1976). Competent, physically attractive women were rated higher than less attractive women, and women as a group were rated lower than men.

Many people claim that these barriers are justified because it's more important for men to have high-level jobs, while women should be home with their children. Others have implied that women are taking jobs away from men. We have already discussed the positive effects of maternal employment on children earlier in this chapter, and according to the Women's Bureau (1972), if all married women stayed home and unemployed men were placed in their jobs, there would be over 15 million unfilled jobs in the United States. Furthermore, most unemployed men do not have the education or the skills to qualify for many of the jobs women hold, such as nursing, teaching, and secretarial work.

Touhey (1974a and b) suggests that the increasing participation by women in high-status "masculine" careers, such as college teaching, law, and medicine, results in a tendency on the part of both men and women to view the prestige and status of these careers as reduced, whereas the increasing participation of men in "feminine" occupations, such as nursing and home economics, increases the prestige of these careers. Hawkins and Pingree (1978), however, in a study based on Touhey's work, found that increasing the number of men in "women's" low-status occupations, such as file clerk, made no difference in the perceived status of these occupations; but the presence of men in high-status "women's" occupations, such as social worker, increased the desirability but not the prestige of the occupations. For high-status "men's" occupations, such as physician, the occupations were rated as even more prestigious but not more desirable with a large proportion of women participating in them; and for low-status "men's" occupations, such as postal clerk, the results were contradictory, a result the investigators interpreted as possibly reflecting the distance of their college-student subjects from such occupations. The results of these two investigations, which were interpreted four years apart, may reflect how attitudes are changing about men and women in the work world; that is, high-status "women's" occupations are becoming more desirable as more men enter these fields, and the prestige of high-status "men's" occupations is remaining the same or is becoming even higher as qualified women enter them.

Implications for Career Counseling

As we have seen, from the time children enter kindergarten, they are aware of occupational sex typing, or what is "women's work" and what is "men's work," and throughout their educational training, these stereotypes are reinforced by teachers, textbooks, curricula, parents, peers, and sex-biased vocational tests and career information provided by career and guidance counselors.

As career counselors and as mental-health professionals, we are often in positions with individual clients or with institutions to significantly affect the socialization process and to change the concept of occupational stereotyping. Unfortunately, however, there is a lot of evidence that suggests that counselors and other mental-health professionals respond differently to male and female clients. For example, Collins and Sedlacek (1972) found that counselors perceive male and female clients differently, and more often, counselors rate men as having vocational-educational problems and women as having social-emotional problems. Counselors of both sexes respond most positively to clients who have career goals that are "appropriate" for their sex (Thomas and Stewart, 1971; Abramowitz et al., 1975), and both male and female counselors tend to use sex-biased and inaccurate vocational tests and information (Bingham and House, 1973). Male counselors are often less accurately informed about important factors relating to sex-biases than female counselors; that is, they are less likely to be aware of differences in the career-development process for men and women or to know about the increasing numbers of women entering and remaining in the labor force or to be aware of sex-biases in widely used tests. However, neither male nor female counselors accurately perceive the work values of men and women, and they tend to underestimate the effect of sex differences in client career choice (McCarthy, 1973). Many professionals who have the greatest opportunity to intervene in the sex-biased career-development process are misinformed, especially about women and work, and tend to devote more time and energy to the vocational problems of men and to the social problems of women. What can we as mental-health professionals do to remedy this situation?

In order to provide effective career counseling, we must obviously be aware of our own biases and the sex-biases in the tests and materials we use. We must consider men and women as equally deserving of career-planning assistance and not assume that a woman who wants career information is different from a man who wants similar help. While it is true that clients sometimes use the topic of careers as a way of seeking counseling for other types of problems, we should not hold different expectations about underlying emotional problems based upon the sex of the client. Similarly, even though female counselors are more often aware of sex-related issues in occupational development and choice, the sex of the counselor is not as important as his or her ability to counsel both men and women in an unbiased way. Mental-health professionals should encourage institutions to develop and expand career-development programs to enhance career development for both sexes. Career-planning programs at the high school and college levels have been demonstrated to increase levels of knowledge about career development and to significantly change attitudes, especially in women, about career possibilities (McEwen, 1975). In addition, professionals can help students form discussion groups about mutual career concerns, lecture to groups about the different career problems for men and women, and instigate appropriate curriculum changes to eliminate sex biases. Since we are aware that nontraditional role models have powerful influences on both sexes, we can present role models directly, for example, by bringing in guest speakers who are themselves working in nontraditional careers, or we can use films or printed materials to present nontraditional role models indirectly.

As professionals, we need to be aware that career development for women is usually different from career development for men, and we must educate ourselves about women's special career needs. As we discussed earlier in this chapter, women do not typically develop a strong sense of identity with occupations and careers, and when they ask for career counseling, they may not be ready to choose a career but rather to begin developing a life plan that will include a career in the future. Women are less likely than men to have been socialized to expect to provide for their own physiological and safety needs, and consequently, they are often less likely than men to be ready to deal with such higher-order needs as self-expression or self-actualization. As Harmon (1977) maintains, it is often useless to try to focus on career choice for women until they have resolved their perceived conflicts of achievement and self-esteem versus belonging and esteem from others. The implied forced choice between marriage and career needs to be eliminated and the option to combine the two should be explored with both women and men.

It is important to assess for each client where he or she is in the stages of career development and to assess which needs he or she is gratifying at the present time. Then the counselor can help the client realistically form a career plan. For example, if a woman or a man is only able to obtain a low-paying job that will barely cover food and safety needs, it would not be reasonable to talk to this client about self-expression or career choices. Rather, the person could be helped to establish a realistic plan that might include ways of learning appropriate skills or receiving the education necessary to progress to the next stage of occupational development. We will have to vary our career-counseling techniques according to the needs of our individual male and female clients or the process of career counseling will be frustrating for everyone involved.

Brooks (1978) has pointed out the special career problems for "reentry women," women who return to the work force after spending several years in the conventional roles of wife and mother. These may be older women whose children have left home or they may be younger women whose youngest child has entered school. They may also be women of any age who are divorced or widowed. According to Brooks, the stages of reentry are two: preparation and decision making. During the preparation phase, the woman needs to be helped to deal with possible psychological blocks, such as low self-confidence, role conflict, and guilt, that prevent commitment to exploring new roles and options. During the decision-making phase, the woman needs help in assessing her abilities and interests and in implementing her goals and options. Brooks also feels that before a reentry woman can fully commit herself to a career, she needs to share her thinking with her family and to have her family involved in the counseling process. Counselors should be prepared to help women who enter counseling at any stage, whether it is a very early stage of vague discontent or a later developmental stage of lack of specific knowledge about a career field, and counselors also need to recognize that the confusion and depression that many reentry women experience are often caused by their present life situations and are not necessarily neurotic.

As mental-health professionals, we can provide career-counseling services to individual clients or to groups of clients, and we can help increase the scope of counselor education by providing relevant course work and group experiences for trainees. We can help employers and placement offices combat discrimination in interviewing and hiring processes, either by providing information about sex biases or by reporting and taking appropriate action after receiving evidence of discriminatory practices. In personnel testing, applicants commonly take a battery of tests to determine the "best" person for a certain position, even though many of the tests used are biased. We have assumed for many years that there are certain personality characteristics that predict success in various careers and that we can use tests to determine these characteristics. There is evidence, however, that indicates that, at least for men, prior employment history may be the best predictor of job success (Schaffer, 1976), and jobs often affect a person's personality more than the person affects the particular job (Kohn and Schooler, 1973). Therefore, we should use information other than test results, when possible, when trying to match people and careers, especially since many of the tests are sex biased and provide barriers to the employment of women.

Case Study Example

Karen J is a forty-three-year-old married woman who makes an appointment with you to discuss her career possibilities. Karen has returned to school after twenty-three years as a housewife and mother and has just completed her undergraduate degree in business administration. She is in the process of applying for jobs in administration or personnel work.

During the session, Karen expresses her frustration and disappointment about her search for a suitable job. She has written several letters and has contacted several personnel offices without success. When she has been able to schedule an interview, she has consistently been asked about her secretarial skills and her willingness to accept a low-status, low-paying job, such as file clerk. When she has indicated that she is not interested in such a job and that she is trained and educated for administrative work, she has been told that since she has little or no experience in administration, she will be required to "start at the bottom" and work her way up into an administrative position.

Karen states that all but one of the people who have interviewed her so far have been men and that she has been told that she is too old to be just starting out in the business world and that she should be at home "enjoying" her free time now that her children are in college. She feels that in some cases the men were telling her, not very subtly, that she would be more likely to be hired if she were younger and consequently more attractive to the men interviewing her. The one woman who interviewed her was somewhat more friendly to her, but she also indicated that Karen should expect to have to work her way up, as she, the interviewer, had had to do, and not expect to begin work in a professional position.

Karen is beginning to doubt that her college degree has any value since she has been able to secure part-time secretarial work throughout her marriage without any degree and now is being offered the same level of job. She is also beginning to doubt her own ability, even though she maintained an A-average in her college work and has outstanding references from her professors. She expressed concern that she may be making a bad impression in the interviews and wonders what she is doing wrong.

During the session, Karen also indicates that she is receiving little support from her husband and children, who feel it is not necessary for her to find a job. Her husband does not have a college education, and Karen feels he is threatened by her success in school and the possibility that she could earn as much or more money than he does. Her children are somewhat embarrassed that she returned to college at the same time that they are attending college, and they have expressed resentment about her excellent grades and her leaving her "responsibilities" in their home. Karen feels that her husband and children not only do not want her to work, but also are pleased that she is having difficulty finding a suitable job. She is also discouraged because most of the men and some of the women who graduated with the same degree as hers have found jobs.

As a career counselor, think about how you might be able to assist Karen. Depending upon your own biases and values, you might choose different ways to work with her. What are your feelings about her? Do you think she is qualified for the type of job she is seeking or would you recommend that she accept a different level of job? From what you know about her, how do you feel about her as a person? Think about how you might react differently to her if she were a man instead of a woman or if she were twenty-three instead of forty-three. Do you believe she is emotionally ready for employment? Would you suggest supportive counseling to help her deal with her feelings of frustration and her disappointment with her husband and family? Would you be more or less likely to suggest supportive counseling if she were a man?

Instead of or along with recommending supportive counseling, you might choose to help her with the job-interview process through role-playing techniques and feedback about the effects of her behavior. You might also help her locate additional community-resource information about employment positions or suggest the possibility of additional education in her chosen field. What is probably most important is that you relate to her in a nonbiased way and that you do not hold different expectations for her because of her sex or age. At the same time, you need to be aware of the job discrimination she is facing as a middle-aged woman and to help her learn the appropriate skills to deal effectively with the sex-role stereotypes that are preventing her from finding employment.

In this chapter, we have examined the different processes of career development and career choice for women and men. In the next chapter, we will turn our attention to a discussion of marriage and its effect on mental health.

6

Marriage and Mental Health

Love and Marriage

In American society, marriage is considered a traditional institution, but, as some comedians have asked, who wants to live in an institution? The answer seems to be that almost all of us do, since almost all men and women in the United States get married at least once during their lives. Unfortunately, many people seem to regard marriage as a confining relationship, and their dissatisfaction is reflected in the ever-increasing divorce rate.

In our society, most men marry, but they don't have to marry in order to fulfill the requirements of their stereotyped sex roles. Women, on the other hand, are expected to marry, and they are usually considered deviant if they are not married by the time they reach age twenty-five, or even worse, thirty. Many people view marriage as an entrapment for men but as the ultimate success for women. Jokes about marriage center around women tricking men into marriage and then men having to put up with the consequences. For example, a poor but often repeated joke, "Take my wife,—please!" is never turned around to be, "Take my husband—please!" Only the first is considered at all funny by most people. Similarly, "Bigamy is having one wife too many. Monogamy is the same," wouldn't make many people laugh if the word "husband" replaced the word "wife." It's not funny when women express dissatisfaction with marriage, even though it's considered funny when men do.

We get married for a variety of reasons: We are in love and want to make the love relationship permanent, we are seeking companionship and want someone who will always be there to do things with us or care for us, we want to be accepted by the rest of society and have children, and we often want stability in our lives and an escape from the fear of being alone. Through marriage relationships, most of us hope to find both security and enduring love-friendships.

Unfortunately, in many marriages, romantic love as an exciting, caring feeling diminishes over time. Historians have concluded that combining love and marriage will always extinguish the love. The early Greeks and Romans, for example, almost all married, but the men weren't expected to love their wives, just to provide for them and protect them. Romantic love was reserved for mistresses and often, in the case of the Greeks, for other men and boys. Similarly, during the Victorian era and during virtually every other era in history, men and women have had lovers but these lovers have not usually been their wives or their husbands. Schlesinger (1966) has written that love and marriage are both endangered species when they are combined, and that the American attempt to combine passion and marriage has only led to "hypocrisy" and "hysteria."

Nevertheless, there is really no evidence to suggest that marriage as an enduring institution in our society is in any particular danger. Most people who are disappointed in marriage either talk about a "mature" kind of love based upon respect and responsibility and acceptance of a certain amount of disillusionment, or they dissolve one marriage and try again in a new marriage relationship. Nevertheless, there *have* been some subtle changes in the way we view marriage. Now, instead of asking what's wrong with women and men who can't adjust to marriage, we have begun asking what's wrong with marriage that so many men and women are dissatisfied.

Marriage Roles

A review of relevant literature by Burke and Weir (1977) indicates that people with happy marriages stress the relationship aspects of marriage, such as their love and concern for each other, rather than situational aspects, such as home, social life, and children, as sources of their happiness. Furthermore, couples who express greater marital satisfaction report communicating openly with each other, expressing feelings freely, and showing sensitivity and understanding for one another's moods and feelings. Not all marriages are happy, however, and in order to understand some of the ways that socialization can affect potential marital happiness, we have to look again at the influences of our stereotyped sex roles.

Pleck (1977) separates marriage roles into two standard roles for men and two possible roles for women, including the male work role, the male family role, the female work role, and the female family role. According to Pleck, a combination of the work-family roles is standard for men and includes the expectation of paid, continuous, full-time work from the end of education to retirement. Men are also expected to utilize their potential to the fullest and to subordinate other roles, including the family role, to the work role. Women, on the other hand, are expected to place their family roles above all other roles and to assume major responsibility for the home and children. Women are allowed to assume the work role as well as long as it doesn't interfere with their marital relationships, the psychological well-being of their children, or the performance of their other family roles. Consequently, many women find themselves in a double bind. If they don't work, they have a good chance of coming down with the "housewife syndrome," which includes such symptoms as depression, insomnia, stomach aches, and other psychosomatic ailments. If they do work, they may be able to avoid these symptoms, but they will also have to coordinate two full-time roles.

For women, unlike men, marriage and work often cause serious conflicts. Walker (1973) has found that even when both husband and wife are employed full-time, husbands do only about one-third of the family work that wives do. Furthermore, although husbands' family time does increase slightly when their wives are employed and a child under the age of two is present, in most situations they contribute about the same time to family tasks—1.6 hours per day —whether their wives are employed or not. Contrary to popular belief, Vanek (1974) found that most American husbands do not share the responsibilities of household work and that most of their "help" consists of doing the shopping or washing the dishes. Furthermore, working wives are no more likely to have paid help than nonemployed wives, and they use their weekends to catch up on their cleaning and family responsibilities. The average American husband uses the weekends to do odd chores and catch up on his rest, and as the family grows larger the husband does *less* housework and cooking and is even less involved in child care.

According to Tavris and Offir (1977), the American father spends an average of only twelve minutes a day with his children. It's interesting that there is considerable discussion of the possible adverse effects of a mother's employment on her children, but there has been little consideration of the effects of a father's employment.

May not his degree of involvement with his work also be harmful to his children? So far, the idea of paternity leave has not often been taken seriously by either men or women. And, according to most of the evidence, a shift of the husband's energies from work to the family, when it has been evident at all, has been dishearteningly slow. The implications here are important. As we noted in Chapter 5, when fathers do help more with household tasks, their behavior can significantly change the sex-role attitudes of their children. As a side note, it is interesting that more men than women express the attitude that wives should be responsible for the sex-role socialization of their daughters, whereas more women than men feel there should be shared responsibility for the socialization of both their sons and their daughters (Araji, 1977).

According to some surveys, young married women report being the happiest group of either sex of any age (Campbell, 1975), but several years after marriage they report being unhappy and dissatisfied with their lives. Nevill and Damico (1977), for example, found that married women between the ages of twenty-five and thirty-nine express more unhappiness and role conflict than married women either younger or older than themselves. Birnbaum (1975) interviewed three groups of intelligent women, fifteen to twenty-five years after they had graduated from college. She divided the women into three groups: women who had married, had children, and had not worked since marriage; women who had married, had children, and were employed Ph.D.'s; and women who were single and were employed Ph.D.'s. She found that of the three groups, the homemakers report being the unhappiest. These women have the lowest self-esteem, feel the least attractive, and often report feeling lonely. They miss creative involvement and feel the most incompetent, even at child care and getting along with people. The married professionals are happier with their marriages than the housewives who devote all of their time to their families, and the only thing the married professional women complain about is not having enough time to do all of the things they want to do. While the single professional women also indicate that they are often lonely and do not feel especially attractive, they report significantly more self-esteem and satisfaction with their lives than the women who are housewives. However, even though married professional women report more marital happiness and satisfaction than unemployed married women, the majority of these women, as well as their husbands, expect the wife's career to be subordinate to the husband's career, and for the wife to place her family role ahead of her career (Bryson et al., 1976). Apparently, even professional career women must tolerate "domestication" in order to maintain a satisfactory marital relationship (Poloma and Garland, 1971).

Power Relationships

Very few marriages are truly democratic or "egalitarian" in the sense that the husband and wife have equal status and power to make important decisions. Even in the Poloma and Garland study (1971), which investigated the relationships of married professional couples, in all of the couples except one the wife was responsible for the household and family tasks, and the husband was responsible for providing the family with status and income. Most of the wives in this study were expected to value their husband's career over their own and to follow him wherever he went, even if it meant giving up their own career opportunities.

In a well-known series of studies, Blood and Wolfe (1960) investigated the balance of power in marriage and found that husbands usually control most of the important power decisions in the family, even though wives have some lesser decision-making power, for example, in deciding how much money the family needs for food each week. According to Blood and Wolfe, the greater the husband's occupational prestige and social status, and the higher his income, the more power he has to make decisions. Blood and Wolfe claim that this superior power of high-status husbands is not due to coercion but to the recognition by both husband and wife that the husband is the one best qualified to make the important decisions in the family. Also, the more education the husband has, especially if his education exceeds his wife's education, the greater his power.

According to Gillespie (1971), in order for the wife to gain a more even balance of power in the marital relationship she must participate in the work force, her education must be superior to that of her husband, and her participation in organizations, such as clubs and civic groups, must exceed his. Women who work have more family power than women who are unemployed, regardless of race or class. The number of years the wife has worked also affects the balance of power, and the longer she has worked the more powerful she is. The stages of the life cycle also apparently affect the marital power distribution, and in the early, childless, stage of marriage, the husband and wife are more nearly equal in decision-making power, especially if the wife is working. With birth of children, however, the husband gains a substantial amount of marital power and the wife has substantially less. As the children grow up, the wife gradually regains some of the decision-making power, especially if she returns to work. Gillespie maintains that power is not the result of individual contributions to the marriage relationship, but is a consequence of the low value and prestige placed on household tasks by society. Even when wives do have decision-making power in their marriages, they often pay a high price for this power. In a study by Meyer and Lewis (1976), as wives were perceived by their husbands to make more decisions, they were perceived as being more dominant, but also as being less loving and affectionate.

There are factors other than employment and education that influence the balance of power in a marriage. Although marriage is ordinarily considered a relationship entered freely by both partners and both are assumed to have equal rights and duties, there are legal differences in most marriage contracts that grant men power over their wives. For example, in many states the husband is legally entitled to his wife's household services, and she cannot be paid for her work. The husband in return must provide his wife with food and shelter and other necessities according to his income level. Furthermore, most wives are not entitled to freedom of movement, and the husband has the legal right to decide where the family will live. If he decides to move, she is obliged to go with him or he can charge her with desertion. Until fairly recently, a woman was required by law to change her last name after marriage and to use her husband's name when applying for credit or buying property, even if she had her own source of independent income.

Sex Roles in Bed

In many states, a husband can legally force his wife to have sexual intercourse with him, because it is considered the "right" of the husband and the "duty" of the wife. By this legal definition, a husband cannot be accused of raping his wife, even though the same act if committed against any other woman would be a felony. Theoretically, the husband also has the "duty" to have intercourse with his wife, but this cannot normally occur against his will. According to Keller (1974), women do have sexual power and even though this power has no legal basis, it can be used by women as a way of obtaining more decision-making power in the marriage. Keller refers to this as "erotic" power and describes it as the ability to arouse, withhold, or gratify sexual desire in men. Keller maintains that when wives have been forced to depend upon their husbands economically and legally they have often retaliated by making their husbands dependent upon them erotically. Wives can also retaliate by remaining unresponsive to their husband's sexual advances and passively accepting intercourse.

Despite recent changes in attitudes about sex roles, as we noted in Chapter 3, the behavior of men and women in sexual relationships is still very consistent with sex-role stereotypes. Men are supposed to be assertive and active and have the power in sexual relationships, as well as most of the responsibility for the success of these relationships. According to Pietropinto and Simenauer (1977), however, most men report that they like sexually assertive women and generally respond favorably to women assuming more power in the sexual relationship. When they were asked "What is the most unpleasant aspect of sex for you?", the vast majority of men answered "having an unresponsive partner," while only a small minority answered "women making demands." According to a recent investigation by Hite (1976), however, although many women report that they would like to be more sexually assertive, they believe that most men don't like assertive women, and they express hesitancy about assuming more power or responsibility in the sexual relationship. Since both of these investigations reflect attitudes and self-reports of behavior, we have no way of assessing whether or not actual behavior changes are occurring in bed and affecting the marital power structure. It seems reasonable to assume, however, that wives who are assertive sexually are also more likely to be assertive in other facets of the marital relationship and to share more power with their husbands than wives who are sexually passive or unresponsive. Masters and Johnson (1975) have concluded that sex used to be something a man did "to" a woman and then it became something a man did "for" a woman. According to these investigators, only recently has sex started to be something a man does "with" a woman.

Marriage and Mental Health

Burke and Weir (1977) have investigated some of the ways that husbands and wives can work together to share some of the power and responsibility in their marriage relationships and to provide a "mental-hygiene" function in marriage. They found that couples who were most satisfied with their marriages tended to select one another as first choice of helper under situations of stress and expressed greater satisfaction with the helping relationship they established. Both men and women who reported greater satisfaction with their job situations described their spouses as more satisfactory helpers and confidantes. Overall, wives were usually more active than their husbands in initiating helping communication and were more likely to turn to their husbands when they needed to discuss their problems, whereas their husbands were more likely to turn to other people. The couples who were older and had been married longer showed a decrease in communication and a diminished level of helping activity, and older wives, especially, indicated they would rather talk to someone other than their husbands. The introduction of children into the family also resulted in less helping behavior for both partners, but the greater the job pressures for either husband or wife, the more likely the partners were to disclose their problems and tensions to each other. Burke and Weir concluded that open communication in marriage and helping behavior by both the husband and the wife can positively influence the quality of marital life and reduce the possibility that accumulated tensions will become emotional symptoms. They further proposed that mental-health professionals need to become more aware of the potential "mental-hygiene" function of communication between husbands and wives and to be aware of the importance of marital-partner helping behavior in creating happy marriages.

Bernard (1972) has stated that men and women get into marriage as they get into bed, that is, with different desires and expectations. Overall, she has found that married men are healthier in all respects than single men, but that married women have more problems than single women. According to Bernard, single men commit more crimes and are more likely to commit suicide than married men, whereas married men are more likely to have higher-status jobs and higher incomes than single men. Married women, however, tend to have more emotional and physical symptoms than single women, and Bernard concludes that marriage may be hazardous to women's health. Another possible interpretation, however, is that at least some women who *choose* to remain single may be psychologically stronger to begin with than women who choose to get married. In another investigation, Gove and Tudor (1973) compared the mental health of married men and women and found that for every category of mental illness married women were less healthy than married men. However, for single, divorced, and widowed men and women, the men in all of these categories tended to have higher rates of mental illness than the women (Gove, 1972). These investigators concluded that at least in terms of mental illness, being married is considerably more advantageous for men than for women, whereas being single is more advantageous for women than for men.

Implications for Counseling and Therapy

Most men and women believe in romantic love and in the possibility of establishing a marriage relationship with an "ideal" person who will make their lives happy and worthwhile. Many of these people are disappointed and disillusioned when marriages don't measure up to their idealized images, however, and they often blame themselves or their spouses for their dissatisfaction and unhappiness. When we examine these expectations for marriage, it does not seem surprising that so many marriages fail or become extremely stressful for the men and women involved. As mental-health professionals, you are probably often in contact with unhappy individuals and couples who are seeking relief from some of their marriage-related symptoms and problems. Depending upon your levels and types of training and your own personal feelings about marital relationships and sex roles, there are many types of techniques and approaches you can utilize to provide services to your clients. Similarly, clients have a wide variety of professionals to choose from, including psychologists, psychiatrists, social workers, members of the clergy, and those represent themselves exclusively as marriage counselors. Not to be overlooked are the "celebrity" sources, such as Ann Landers and Joyce Brothers, as well as several other columnists and representatives of the media, who also diagnose and prescribe and refer for many anonymous clients. Some of the therapy approaches that you, as a professional, might choose to utilize include individual therapy with one or both of the marital partners, marital therapy where both partners are seen together by the same therapist or by cotherapists, married-couples group therapy, family therapy which includes the children, or group therapy which does not include both husbands and wives in the same group. Depending upon your individual experiences and orientation, you probably prefer one or more of these approaches and have strong feelings about the use of others.

Case Study Example

Mary and George R have requested to meet with you as a couple. They have been married for fifteen years and have a daughter who is twelve years old and a son who is nine. Mary is thirty-five and has a college degree in education. She worked as a sixth-grade teacher for three years prior to the birth of her daughter, and she did not return to work after the children were born. She is active in clubs and volunteer organizations within the community, and she has just been elected president of her PTA group. George is forty years old and is a successful dentist who earns approximately $45,000 per year. He belongs to an athletic club, but he does not belong to other organizations within the community.

Mary and George have stated that they have been experiencing marital difficulties and that they are also concerned about their children. When they arrive for their appointment, Mary appears nervous and upset and George appears outwardly calm but somewhat uncomfortable. As the session progresses, you learn that both Mary and George feel that their marital relationship is deteriorating and that they have essentially stopped communicating with each other except to discuss matters concerning their children. They do not socialize very often as a couple, and except for the children, they appear to have different interests and groups of friends. Also their sexual relationship is no longer satisfying and they have not had sexual contact for several months.

Mary states that during the last three or four years she has felt that George has had little interest in her as a person and that he has been much more involved in his work than in his home life. She indicates that she feels neglected and rejected, but that she feels she and George have an obligation to work out their problems and differences for the sake of their children. She states that their marriage is not a bad marriage but that she knows it is not really a satisfying relationship at the present time for either of them. George states that he agrees with Mary that their relationship has been deteriorating during the last several years but that he disagrees that it is because of his interest in his work. He indicates that he has felt himself growing away from Mary and that he feels that they have both changed considerably during the fifteen years that they have been married. He feels they no longer have much in common besides the children and that they are wasting each other's lives by remaining married only for the sake of the children.

As George talks, Mary begins to cry, and she states that she doesn't want a divorce and that she doesn't want to be left alone. She states that she feels George married her "for better or for worse" and that he has an obligation to remain with the family. She further states that she loves George and she feels that their marriage can be saved. George states that he loves Mary "as a friend and as a sister" but that he thinks they would be better off living separately. He says that he loves his children and can not really conceive of living without them but that he is willing to give everything he owns to Mary and their children as long as he is able to see the children frequently once they have been divorced. George also states that he is in love with another woman and that his relationship with her is more satisfying to him personally and sexually than his relationship with Mary has ever been. Mary cries harder as George talks about his other relationship and states that the situation is unfair and humiliating to her and that she feels that George is only interested in someone else because of sex. She feels that they should try harder to improve their own sexual relationship and that, with help, they can salvage their marriage. She further states that she would be willing to move to a new location so that they could "start over" without the other woman being available to "seduce" George and to turn him away from her and from his obligations to his children.

Following this initial consultation session you, as a mental-health professional, must decide how or if you will work with Mary and George. Depending upon your feelings about each of them and upon your personal orientation, you may choose to work with them as a couple or to work with them individually, or you may choose to work with one of them or neither of them. Think about your feelings about Mary and George as individuals. Do you have strong positive or negative feelings about one or the other or both of them? Do you think their marital relationship can be or should be salvaged? Do you agree with Mary that she and George have an obligation to try to work out their problems and differences? Do you feel any sympathy or empathy for her or does she make you at all angry or impatient? Think about how you reacted when George stated that he was in love with another woman. Did your feelings about him change in any way? Would you have felt differently if Mary had been the one who stated that she was in love with someone else? You may be aware that you feel differently about Mary or George and that you may like one of them better than the other.

Depending upon your own feelings about marital relationships and sex roles, you may choose to work with one or both of them or to refer their case to someone else.

Regardless of the approach you use or whether you are a man or a woman, you will provide the most effective services for your clients if you are aware of your own feelings about sex roles in marital relationships and are relatively free from the prejudice that middle-class marriage and family life are the best and only acceptable ways of living. You also need to keep in touch with information about current approaches to marital counseling and therapy.

Examples of Treatment Approaches

Rice and Rice (1977) maintain that it is rare to find a male therapist who can effectively conduct nonsexist marital therapy. They argue that unless he has himself been in a nontraditional relationship with a woman or has had to restructure his own marriage, a male therapist is more likely than a female therapist to hold values and biases that only reinforce sterotyped marriage roles. In order to prevent sex-role biases in marital therapy, Rice and Rice recommend an approach where two therapists, one a man and one a woman, both work with the couple from the start of the therapy process. The relationship between the therapists must be as egalitarian as possible; for example, they should have equal professional titles and status and should regard one another as peers. Therapy should take place in a neutral office or room rather than in one of the therapist's offices, and both therapists need to guard against assuming sex-stereotyped patterns of behavior; for example, the male therapist providing interpretations and the female therapist responding to feelings.

Ellis (1974), on the other hand, asserts that the vast majority of women and men today seem to suffer from fairly serious love and sex difficulties, and the approach a mental-health professional uses to deal with these relationship problems is more important than the sex of the therapist. According to Ellis, either women or men who tend to make love not merely an important part of their lives but their whole existence, are exhibiting severe symptoms of disturbances which he has labeled "love slobbism." Love slobs are people who believe they must be part of an intimate couple in order to exist and that they must have someone who loves them as long as they live. When their attempts to nail down love guarantees appear to be failing, love slobs typically make themselves feel desperately lonely, depressed, worthless, and sometimes suicidal.

Ellis maintains that love slobbism is an emotional consequence (C) in the ABC's of rational-emotive psychology. It usually follows an activating event (A), such as disappointment in a marriage relationship. In order to help the client deal effectively with his or her problem, the therapist concentrates on helping the client understand his or her belief system (B), which interprets and evaluates the activating events. For example, a woman who is unhappy with her marriage relationship (A) becomes frustrated, angry, depressed, and hurt (C) because she has been thinking that she will never be able to maintain a successful relationship with her husband or be worthy of his love (B). According to Ellis, only the woman's irrational interpretations of the situations make it demeaning and depressing, and what the therapist does is to try to induce her to dispute (D) her irrational beliefs that everything is awful and that she is a bad person. In order to help people dispute their irrational beliefs the therapist teaches them that there aren't any absolute "shoulds," "musts," "have-to's," or "necessities" in their lives and that "ten-thousand it-would-be-better's never equal a single should." For example, no one "must" have someone else's complete and absolute guaranteed love in order to accept himself or herself and live a reasonably happy existence. It might be preferable if one's marital partner could be more ideal in many ways, but it's not a necessity.

Similarly, Ellis believes that clients can be taught to criticize their own *behavior* and the *behavior* of their partners without damning themselves or their partners as totally worthless human beings.

Chesler (1971) does not agree with Ellis and has concluded that male therapists should not attempt to treat female patients. She maintains that marriage and psychotherapy are the two major socially approved institutions for women and that they both isolate women from other women and are ways of socially controlling and oppressing women. She sees psychotherapy as encouraging women to talk but not to act while the therapist subtly controls what the woman says. According to Chesler, both husbands and male therapists tend to view women as children and have been conditioned to view women as inferior, castrating, and alien to themselves. She doesn't see how a female patient can be free of the stereotypes of a sexist society with a male therapist, and she recommends that only women therapists treat women patients. Chesler also maintains that women therapists can be as sex-biased as men if they have not yet realized that they themselves are oppressed as women and if they view marriage and children as fulfillment for all women. However, they are more likely to be aware of sex-role biases than male therapists.

Seidenberg (1977) believes that what usually appear to be problems of marriage are really problems of individuals and that marriage counseling may be dealing only with the symptoms rather than the causes of the problems. He maintains that persons, not marriages, are worth saving and that the best approach is to treat individuals rather than a marriage or marriage partners. According to Seidenberg, there may be a legitimate need for "mediators" in modern society, but he would not equate them with therapists, and he asserts that treating marital partners together or alternately makes implicit value judgments about marriage. He contends that psychoanalysis, which deals with the needs and anxieties of an individual rather than a marriage, or a family, or a community, is the most effective method of treatment for all individuals, if the therapist is aware of his or her own values and biases. For example, in psychoanalysis when a male client does not express a desire to compete, or achieve, or dominate at home or at the office, therapists often explain the client's behavior on the basis of the Oedipus complex; that is, he is fearful of competing with his father. According to Seidenberg, therapists must become aware of the fact that sex roles are changing and it is no longer permissible to assume automatically that a man who doesn't follow the traditional male role is necessarily neurotic or "sick." Similarly, the "anatomy-as-destiny" tradition in psychoanalysis must give way to a more realistic appraisal of sex roles and stereotypes. Seidenberg acknowledges that there are too many psychoanalysts who are "unaware" and take pride in their aloofness, and he compares these analysts to medieval monks who fear that contact with the contemporary world will be contaminating. Nevertheless, he maintains that psychoanalysis can be the most effective treatment procedure available, and other forms of intervention, such as marital counseling, are really managerial techniques and do not qualify as therapy, even though they may sometimes be helpful to the clients involved.

Alsbrook (1976), on the other hand, has concluded that positive results can be obtained from marital counseling if the therapists are aware of the effects of power positions within the marriage relationship. According to Alsbrook, if therapists attempt to get both partners back into their "appropriate places" within the marriage, this type of counseling will become less and less effective. Rather, the therapists need to approach the conflicted marriages from the perspective of subordinate and superordinate relationships and help the husbands and wives become aware of these roles within their marriages. The search for a villain in problem marriages is usually a waste of time, Alsbrook maintains, since men in our society have been socialized into the oppressor role just as women have been socialized into the oppressed role. Instead, the therapist must help both partners take more responsibility to elevate their marriage to a rewarding level characterized by equality and mutual acceptance and open communication.

Counseling the Divorced or Widowed

As we noted previously, the approach you prefer when counseling men and women with marital-related problems depends upon such factors as your training orientation and your own personality. You probably also respond somewhat differently to various clients depending upon the needs and values of the clients themselves. For example, a client who contacts you individually and is seeking help in understanding his or her marital-related problems may be looking for a different kind of help than a husband and a wife who want to participate together in counseling. Similarly, people who are going through a divorce procedure or who are already divorced when they contact you for help may have interpersonal problems that are related to their marriages, but they are not in the same life situation as people who are still married and are interested in trying to work out their problems within the marriage.

Aslin (1978) maintains that people who are divorced are similar in many ways to people who are widowed. Both the "death" of a marriage relationship and the death of a spouse result in men and women becoming single again, and often divorced and widowed men and women are not prepared to be single. Bohannan (1970) maintains that there are at least six processes which occur after people become single again, including emotional, legal, economic, parental, social, and psychic processes, and that a therapist or counselor must often help clients deal with one or more of these processes.

The emotional phase of becoming single again may be experienced differently by clients depending upon whether they are men or women as well as upon their own unique life situations. Gettlemen and Markowitz (1974) maintain that our society reinforces the belief that becoming single again will be a traumatic and devastating experience and, consequently, many people do feel this way. Typically, pain and suffering accompany the death of the marital relationship and the loss of a person's familiar role as a husband or a wife. According to Aslin (1978), since women traditionally identify more closely with their family and marriage roles than men do, they often find their single status more traumatic and experience a greater sense of loss. Counselors often must help both women and men accept and adjust to their new roles and not reinforce society's expectations for a sense of failure and lost identity. Similarly, the counselor needs to be aware that not all divorced or widowed clients experience the emotional process at the same time. Some have completed the emotional separation from their former marital partner before they turn to counseling for help, while others may be emotionally dependent long after.

During the legal and economic phases of becoming single again, clients may need referrals to appropriate sources where they can obtain accurate information about their new status. Counselors can refer their clients to appropriate professionals, such as attorneys and accountants, since it is not advisable for counselors to dispense legal advice themselves. At the same time, however, counselors can help their clients deal with their feelings about these processes and can explore with the women the necessities and opportunities for becoming independent in a variety of ways, for example, in seeking employment or applying for credit.

If the former husband or wife has custody of minor children, he or she will most likely need help with the parental process. The woman may find herself as a mother without a father (or a full-time father) for her children, or she may find herself as a mother without "full-time" children, in the relatively rare instances that the father is awarded custody. Similarly, the man may find himself as a father without a mother (or at least a full-time mother) for his children or as a father without full-time children. According to Aslin, the basis for many problems with these new roles is the myth that children are damaged by not having two full-time parents, regardless of the quality of the parenting. Single-again parents need help in understanding that their new status will not necessarily have negative effects on their children, and as Bohannan (1970) maintains, since children tend to mirror their parents' emotions, the easier the readjustment is for the single-again parents, the easier it will be for their children.

During the social process, counselors can help clients adjust to being single in our couples-oriented society and can help them cope with feelings of lost identity as a member of a pair and feelings of anxiety related to discovering a new identity as a single person. Similarly, during the psychic process, single-again clients typically have reactions including loneliness, fear, and despair, and counselors can provide support during these times. Furthermore, Aslin (1978) maintains that the sex of the counselor or therapist as well as his or her own marital status may significantly affect treatment with single-again clients, especially if the therapist's own security is threatened by the discussion of divorce or the death of a spouse. Counselors and therapists may be forced to deal with their own feelings of loneliness and alienation or dissatisfaction with unhappy marriages. Mental-health professionals must also be alert for symptoms of severe psychological stress, such as severe anxiety or depression, which may indicate that a particular client requires more than supportive or directive counseling.

Sex Roles and Mental Illness

In our society, women have higher rates of mental illness than men. Gove and Tudor (1973) looked at the proportion of men and women who were diagnosed as mentally ill as indicated by first admissions to mental hospitals, treatment in outpatient clinics, psychiatric treatment in general hospitals, and treatment for emotional illness in the practices of general physicians. All of these sources indicated that women are more likely to be diagnosed as mentally ill than men. Nearly two of every three patients are women, and for most age groups, women are approximately twice as likely to be perceived as having psychiatric and emotional problems. As we noted in Chapter 5, even the majority of women who ask for help in career counseling are regarded as having emotional problems rather than career difficulties, whereas men who ask for career counseling are regarded as needing vocational and educational guidance. Gove and Tudor also concluded that most people who receive treatment for emotional disorders are treated by physicians within the community without special psychiatric or psychological training, and that more women than men receive this kind of treatment. Linn (1971) reported that general practitioners and internists rate middle-aged housewives as legitimately needing tranquilizing medication more often than men, and Rosen et al. (1972) concluded that two-thirds of the patients perceived as mentally ill in general medical clinics are women.

Surveys from psychiatric and psychological clinics indicate that women remain in psychotherapy longer than men and that women are prescribed significantly more medication for the treatment of emotional symptoms (Abramowitz et al., 1974; National Disease and Therapeutic Index, 1970). In a related study, Stein et al. (1974) asked clinicians to rate hypothetical patients on factors related to diagnosis, prognosis, and treatment recommendations, and found that the identical hypothetical patient was rated as more maladjusted and in need of medication significantly more often when the clinicians believed that the patient was a woman rather than a man. Similarly, a study of psychologists in private practice found that the greatest percentages of the clients for both male and female clinicians consisted of women seen in individual therapy, and that less than 1 percent of the clients of the female clinicians and less than 13 percent of the clients of the male clinicians were men in individual therapy (Pendergrass, 1974). As we noted in Chapter 4, most of the gifted women in the longitudinal study conducted by Terman et al. (1959) did not apply their intelligence and creativity to productive achievement the way most of the gifted men did. It is also interesting to note that these gifted women have had a higher rate of mental illness than would be expected from the general population, whereas the rate for the gifted men has been lower than expected.

While there is evidence that more women than men are diagnosed as mentally ill, several investigators have suggested that the different diagnosis and treatment of women and men may relate more to the attitudes and biases of the clinicians than to actual differences in severity of disturbance for the sexes (Linn, 1971; Stein et al., 1974). Also, as we have noted earlier in this chapter, it is the relatively high rate of diagnosed mental illness in married women that accounts for the higher rates of mental illness among women (Gove, 1972).

Why More Women Are Diagnosed as Mentally Ill

Williams (1977) has proposed that there are several plausible explanations that may account for the higher incidence of perceived mental illness among women, including both biological and sociological explanations. Genetically, women appear stronger than men, since they have fewer genetic defects at birth and are usually developmentally ahead of boys at birth and for several years beyond (Maccoby and Jacklin, 1974). However, women's biology is different in other ways that have been seen as significant for mental health. Because women menstruate and sometimes have mood changes associated with the menstrual cycle, these "raging hormonal imbalances" have often been blamed for the high incidence of mental illness in women, even though, for most women, these physical changes create few psychological problems and often women are not even aware of them (Golub, 1973). Similarly, the process of menopause can be accompanied by severe depression in some middle-aged women, but this depression is apparently caused as much by the socialization process as by actual biological or physical changes (Bart, 1971), and menopause by itself does not explain why more women than men are diagnosed as mentally ill. Gove (1972) further notes that if women are biologically more susceptible to mental illness than men, then all women, instead of only married women, should have higher rates of mental illness than men.

Other explanations are based on sex differences in the socialization process rather than on biological differences. For example, one explanation is based on the different sex roles for women and men. Since many women in our society have a single major role, that of housewife/mother, they value interpersonal relationships and family ties more than men and are more affected by their disruption or loss. Men, on the other hand, usually have two major roles, including achiever in the work world as well as husband/father, and they identify with both roles rather than just one. Even when women are employed, they are likely to hold relatively low-level jobs whose importance is not central to their identity and self-esteem. As we have previously noted, the housewife who works typically not only holds a less satisfying job than her husband, but is also responsible for the vast majority of the household and childrearing tasks, and is usually not positively reinforced for performing these low-status tasks. Bernard (1971, 1973) maintains that the housewife role is boring and frustrating to many women because there are no special requirements for the role and educational levels and abilities are not considered important. The woman's expectations for her marital role are built on stereotypes, and the reality of the role itself results in disillusionment and depression. According to Bernard, the mental health of housewives is "public enemy number one." Another socialized explanation for the high incidence of mental disorders in women is based on the socialization process that encourages women to express their feelings openly and to turn to others for help, whereas men are socialized not to admit to having problems or to having an inability to cope. Therefore, it may be easier for women to seek help and become a patient. Gove (1972), however, again points out that if the higher rates of mental illness for women were only due to these characteristics of the generalized sex roles, all women, rather than only married women, would seek help and be diagnosed as having higher rates of mental illness than men.

Chesler (1973) maintains that women are seen as crazy whether they accept or reject the female sex role. According to Chesler, if a woman accepts the stereotyped role, she's going to become unhappy and depressed, and perhaps even paranoid or frigid. If she seeks treatment, she will be diagnosed as having a neurotic depression or an anxiety neurosis. On the other hand, if a woman rejects the female sex role and becomes aggressive or assertive, she is likely to be diagnosed as schizophrenic. Chesler asserts that mental illness is nothing more than women or men rejecting their stereotyped sex roles. When men are passive and depressed and don't especially want to achieve, they may be diagnosed as schizophrenic, but they will usually not be diagnosed as neurotics. Men and women who reject their sex roles are often diagnosed as severely disturbed, whereas men and women who are dissatisfied within their "appropriate" sex roles are often diagnosed as neurotic or just unhappy. Chesler also maintains that the female role is badly in need of help, but that when women do express emotional stress and unhappiness they often get locked into psychiatric wards and are deprived of their civil rights. She believes more women than men seek help because women are more oppressed by their limited sex roles but that very few women or men are truly "crazy." Rather, they are rebelling against or unhappily acting out their stereotyped sex roles.

Men and Women as Patients

Once men and women have been diagnosed as mentally ill, they are often treated differently in their status as patients. The role of the patient is more compatible with the female sex role than with the male sex role, since being a patient requires an acknowledgment of weakness, dependency, and submission to authority, and men are not "supposed" to exhibit these types of behavior. Howell (1974) found that women fit so naturally into the role of patient that often less concern is given to their specific conditions and health care as compared to men. Mental-health-care professionals and physicians often share common assumptions about the personalities and behavior of women and treat them accordingly. For example, according to Howell, even though breast cancer is the second leading cause of death in women and there is some evidence that breast cancer and psychological stress are related, there is little research being funded or conducted in this area. Women are seen as unreliable sources of their own symptom histories, and their complaints are often considered psychosomatic and uninteresting.

Stein et al. (1976) compared outpatient treatment programs for men and women who were diagnosed as neurotic depressives. Although the women patients rated themselves as more angry than the men on a mood scale, no other differences were found in the levels of stress or the types of needs for the two sexes. Similarly, there were no differences for the variables of age, race, marital status, and education. These investigators found that the women remained in treatment significantly longer than the men, and a significantly higher proportion of the women received some form of antidepressant drugs. When men received medication, it consisted of minor tranquilizers, whereas women were given more potent, mood-elevating drugs. Stein et al. recommended that more investigations are needed to determine the extent to which therapists view men and women within the same diagnostic categories as differing in severity of disturbance and the extent to which different attitudes toward male and female patients are a function of the sex of the therapist.

Other investigators have also found that women receive a disproportionate amount of the drugs that are prescribed and that women receive more potent psychoactive drugs, which affect mental and emotional states, than men do (Brodsky, 1971; Fidell, 1973). Prather and Fidell (1972) conducted a survey of drug advertisements in medical journals and found that advertising can influence the ways that physicians treat women and men. Sex-role stereotypes were reinforced by the drug ads, and both women and men were depicted as recovering from mental illness when they began to exhibit "appropriate" sex-role behavior and attitudes. Psychoactive drugs were described as more appropriate for women than for men and were recommended for different symptoms for the two sexes. For example, psychoactive drugs were recommended for women with symptoms of anxiety, tension, and depression, whereas these drugs were recommended for men with work-related symptoms. Nonpsychoactive drugs were suggested for use with male patients, implying that men have more "real" illnesses than women, whereas women have more "mental" problems.

Chesler (1973) maintains that men and women are treated differently as patients because 90 percent of the professionals in the mental-health field are men and are biased in favor of men and against women. According to Chesler, there are biases inherent in all psychological theories and these biases affect patient treatment. Most basically, the major bias is that everyone is crazy. Chesler asserts that therapists never assume that a person is mentally healthy but instead look for something that is wrong. A related bias is that even though everyone is crazy, women are crazier. Another sex-related bias is that in order for a woman to be a real woman she has to become a mother, and that once a woman becomes a mother, everything is her fault. According to Chesler, as long as the majority of mental-health professionals believe that women patients need to be treated like children and helped to adjust to their "appropriate" sex roles and that men patients have work-related problems, more women than men will be admitted to psychiatric-treatment centers and be receiving treatment for their "crazy" behavior.

In the next chapter, we will examine the process of psychotherapy in greater detail and discuss the concept of nonsexist psychotherapy for women and men.

7

Psychotherapy

Theories and Techniques

The term "psychotherapy" implies the use of psychological techniques by mental-health professionals to alleviate symptoms of emotional disorders or problems in everyday living. Techniques may range from simply giving advice and direction to providing emotional support and making interpretations about feelings and behavior. Many people who receive psychotherapy are not mentally ill or severely disturbed, but are seeking help during periods of stress in their lives, whereas others receive psychotherapy while hospitalized and are unable to function within society. There are many types of psychotherapy, and the term itself does not imply the seriousness of the problem or the length of time required for treatment, and it covers a wide variety of theoretical orientations. The goal of psychotherapy is to provide treatment that results in changes in the person seeking help. These changes may include changes in attitudes and feelings as well as changes in behavior and in the person's ability to function as a mentally healthy member of society. Both men and women are treated in psychotherapy, but as we concluded in Chapter 6, women are the main consumers of these techniques.

Even though more women than men receive psychotherapy, many of the psychotherapy theories and techniques have been criticized as being particularly biased against women and potentially harmful to women. According to many writers, psychotherapy has often reinforced the sex biases of our male-oriented society and has helped maintain the myth that women are innately inferior to men (Barrett et al., 1974; Chesler, 1972). Most theories of personality are based on the behavior of men and only secondarily refer to women in relation to men and as distinctly different from men (Shields, 1975). Freud's psychoanalytic theory has been the most criticized of all personality theories. Psychoanalysis provided the first comprehensive theoretical explanation of sex differences and has had the greatest and most continuous influence on psychotherapy. Even though some feminists have suggested dismissing Freud and his concepts of penis envy and castration anxiety as a sick joke (Deckard, 1975), we cannot dismiss him so easily. Psychoanalytic theory has had too much effect on our thinking and attitudes about women and men and still continues to influence greatly the process of psychotherapy. Even conclusions that Freud himself described as tentative have been extended and misrepresented as a universal theory of the behavior of women (Mitchell, 1974). While a few theories of personality have been developed specifically to deal with both men and women (for example, Karen Horney and Clara Thompson are two psychoanalysts who rejected Freud's views in favor of sociological explanations as determinants of behavior), most theories have discussed the behavior of women only as complementary to the function of men (Shields, 1975).

The personality theory that a particular therapist believes in and uses can affect the type of treatment that his or her clients will receive. If a therapist believes in biological determinism, for example, he or she will assume that a woman's potential is limited by her anatomy and that her most appropriate role is that of wife and mother. On the other hand, a therapist who believes in the effects of the socialization process, or cultural determinism, will assume that the behavior of both women and men is determined by their life-experiences and the sex-role expectations of society rather than by innate, permanent differences between the sexes. Although some feminists have asserted that all men have vested interests in maintaining the secondary status of women in order to continue their dominance and power in our society, and therefore that no man can effectively provide psychotherapy for a woman (Chesler, 1972), a variable that seems at least as important as the sex of the therapist is whether or not the therapist adheres to theories that are obviously biased against women. Furthermore, it is not sufficient to consider only the personality theory of a particular therapist, but also we need to consider the therapist's model of mental health.

Models of Mental Health

Halleck (1971) has observed that no theory of psychotherapy is politically or ethically neutral, and that a therapist is required to take positions on issues that involve the distribution of power within society. According to Rawlings and Carter (1977), there are three models of mental health that a therapist can choose from to express his or her values and beliefs about the behavior of women and men, including (1) the "normative" model, (2) the "androcentric" model, and (3) the "androgynous" model.

The normative model of mental health defines mental health as adherence to stereotyped sex roles. This is the model widely accepted by the general public and prescribed by society. Since role prescriptions are different for men and women, the normative model implies a double standard of mental health. Therapists who utilize this model attempt to help men and women accept and adjust to their "appropriate" sex roles and treat men and women differently.

The androcentric model is a male-centered model of mental health. Even though this model presents only one standard of mental health for both sexes, it is the male standard, and women are encouraged to change and become more "masculine," whereas men are encouraged to maintain their "healthy" sex-role behavior. A therapist using this model of mental health would still treat men and women differently by encouraging men to accept their "appropriate" sex roles and women to incorporate more "male" traits, such as assertiveness and independence, as part of their sex roles. This model of mental health interprets masculine-associated activities and traits as superior and denigrates whatever is considered "feminine."

The androgynous model of mental health is related to the research on androgyny that we discussed in Chapter 3. According to this model, men and women are encouraged to adopt flexible sex roles that are neither "masculine" nor "feminine," but rather are an integration and balance of both. With this model of mental health, there is only one standard for both women and men, and a therapist following this model would treat men and women equally and would have as treatment goals the integration of the best of both female-associated and male-associated characteristics.

As Halleck noted, all systems of psychotherapy contain implicit value systems, and there is no such thing as value-free psychotherapy. Therapist values, both personal and professional, influence value change in their clients and depend upon the therapists' theoretical orientations as well as upon their models of mental health. These values also determine whether therapists are providing sex-biased or nonsexist psychotherapy for their clients.

Stricker (1977) points out that in considering the treatment of people in psychotherapy, it is important to distinguish between sexist therapy and "bad" therapy. For example, a therapist who is insensitive and exploitative will be of no help to either female or male patients and such a therapist's incompetence should be considered a product of general inadequacy rather than sexism. According to Stricker, sexist therapy occurs when men and women are treated differently and the quality of the therapy provided for women is inferior, or when men and women are treated similarly but according to procedures based upon a male standard of mental health.

Sherman et al. (1978) studied a variety of male and female therapists, including psychologists, psychiatrists, and social workers, and found that there were no significant differences among professions in terms of the therapists' attitudes and information about the expected behavior of their patients and clients. They did, however, find significant differences between the two sexes, and found that women were better informed, more liberal, and less stereotyped in their attitudes. Although the trend for both women and men was toward more liberal and less stereotyped attitudes, many therapists showed a lack of pertinent information that could affect the treatment of their clients. For example, in response to the question, "More women than men in this country seek therapy. How would you account for this?" 89 percent of the therapists indicated that a woman's role and social training make it easier for her to seek therapy. More women than men suggested, however, that women are under more stress because of their sex roles. Although 88 percent of the therapists reported that they would "support individual development even if it runs counter to traditional sex-role expectations," 70 percent, and significantly more men than women, were either neutral or thought that marriage or its continuance should be considered an important goal for women in therapy. Similarly, 55 percent of the therapists, again significantly more men than women, were either neutral or agreed with the statement that it is "better for women with young children to be at home." Sherman et al. also found that male therapists were less well informed than female therapists, especially on such topics as sexuality, menstruation, pregnancy, childbirth, and menopause. Both men and women were unfamiliar with the results of many pertinent studies, and 18 percent of the therapists agreed or weren't sure whether victims of rape had been subtly seductive, and 26 percent did not know that most women do not suffer serious psychological consequences following abortion. Another interesting finding was that 71 percent of the therapists thought that the "cure of frigidity" was an important goal for female clients, even though, as the investigators point out, the entire concept of "frigidity" is now being questioned and there may be no such thing as a frigid woman, only a frigid relationship. The investigators concluded that sex bias and sex-role stereotyping are not uncommon in psychotherapy and are more likely to be found among male than female therapists. Both men and women are relatively unaware of information pertaining to sex biases, and therapists often seemed less biased than uninformed.

Sex Variables and Psychotherapy

As we noted previously, the majority of therapists in the mental-health professions are men, and of the relatively few female therapists available, many of the older women were trained in male-dominated training programs and reflect the male model (Rice and Rice, 1973). As we also noted, the majority of the clients seeking treatment are women, and the most common pattern is that of a male therapist treating a female client. Studies have indicated that most men and women seem to prefer having male therapists, even though in recent years feminists have been advocating female therapists for female clients and women are beginning to shift their therapist preferences (Chesler, 1971; Fabrikant, 1974). Helms and Simons (1975) found that when age and sex of therapists were taken into account, clients were influenced by both variables and did not choose a therapist on the basis of sex alone, and Simons and Helms (1976) found that both college and noncollege women preferred female counselors when the counselors were described as working in the area of women's problems. Apparently, the sex of the therapist is no longer the only variable being considered by clients when they choose a therapist, and variables such as race, age, marital status, and experience level are also being evaluated when clients indicate their preferences (Brooks, 1974; Hill, 1975).

Fabrikant (1974) investigated therapist and client perceptions of psychotherapy by having male and female therapists as well as male and female clients respond to a series of questions about the therapy process. The therapists were asked to give their own responses to the questions, and the clients were asked to respond as they thought their therapists would. For the personal and attitudinal questions, it was found that therapists' verbalized attitudes were not always the same as the impressions they conveyed to their clients. For example, on a question regarding marriage, both male and female therapists agreed that neither men nor women need to be married to experience a full and satisfying life, and this attitude was accurately perceived by the clients. However, even though all therapists also agreed that marriage should be a partnership, the female clients felt that the therapists were conveying the attitude that the husband should be dominant in the marital relationship. Similarly, although both male and female therapists agreed that both husbands and wives may have sexual partners other than the spouse, both male and female clients felt that the therapists really believed that the wife should be more dependent upon her husband for sexual gratification than the husband on the wife. On another issue, all therapists agreed that the main goal for a woman in therapy was to select her own life-style, and this goal was accurately perceived by all clients. However, when male therapists also responded that male and female therapists do not differ in their goals for their clients, neither female clients nor female therapists agreed. When Fabrikant asked therapists to select sex-role characteristics that were equally representative of men and women, their clients accurately perceived the therapists' choices. Fabrikant concluded that therapists of both sexes are exhibiting more liberal attitudes, especially toward female clients, and that in many cases this shift in attitudes is being perceived by their clients. Although therapists may be more liberal and ready to change existing sex roles, however, clients may not be as ready to change roles, and according to Fabrikant, this may account for some of the apparent discrepancies between therapist attitudes and client perceptions. There is also an indication that therapists may not be as sexist as some feminists claim and that a shift toward more liberal attitudes is slowly occurring.

When Sherman et al. (1978) asked therapists how they thought the sex of the therapists might influence therapy, 69 percent of the therapists of both sexes thought the sex of the therapist was an important variable. More men (52 percent) than women (33 percent) did not think it was easier for a woman to relate to a female therapist, and psychiatrists of both sexes were more likely than either social workers or psychologists to think that the sex of the therapist had no influence on the therapy process. Rawlings and Carter (1977) maintain that a therapist's personality as well as his or her sex affects the adequacy of therapy and that a therapist's own conflicts and problems can cause him or her to be less adequate as a therapist when dealing with material that is related to these conflicts. Therefore, they conclude that male therapists who have interpersonal problems with women in their own lives might convey unintentional biases about cultural values and sex roles to their female clients. Similarly, female therapists who encourage sex-role stereotypes can be as uncomprehending of women's problems as male therapists, and Queen Bee therapists, as we discussed previously, can be especially damaging to other women since they feel that most other women are inferior and that other women are not really motivated to succeed. Abramowitz and Dokecki (1977) maintain, however, that social class may be a more potent determinant of therapist biases than sex of the therapist, and Oppidisano-Reich (1976) found that the training and orientation of professionals within the mental-health field may have more influence on sex biases than the sex of the therapists. For example, women are rated as more mentally ill than men by psychiatrists of both sexes, but not by psychologists or social workers.

Therapy Issues and Ethics

Rawlings and Carter (1977) disagree with the extreme feminist position that men should never treat women, and they believe instead that nonsexist men who are knowledgeable about women's problems are qualified to treat women and are *more* qualified than women who are sexist in their approach to therapy. Also, some female clients are adamant about having a male therapist, and if this is the case, treatment by a male therapist would be best. At the same time, however, Rawlings and Carter feel there are certain situations in which men should not treat women.

1. A man should not do therapy with an all-female group. Since only female therapists can serve as role models for female clients, a man leading the group would produce a situation in which women are once more exposed to the role model of a powerful man. This situation reinforces dependency and encourages the women to compete for the man's attention.
2. Men who have "rescue fantasies" about women should not do therapy with dependent women whose husbands mistreat them. In

this situation, the woman is often reinforced to become dependent upon the supportive therapist and to transfer her dependency from her husband to the therapist instead of learning to become self-sufficient. Even if she leaves her husband she will have great difficulty leaving therapy.

3. Men should not do therapy with women who are hostile to men. Even though the practice has often been to assign these women to a male therapist in order to work through their hostility, Rawlings and Carter maintain that it would be easier and more productive for a client hostile to men to work first with a female therapist and then, when the client feels prepared, to either include a male cotherapist or have the client participate in a mixed-sex group.

4. Men should not do therapy with women who relate to men primarily in a seductive manner. These women try to appeal to male therapists sexually because they have been socialized to try to be pleasing to men, and they often have very strong dependency needs. The concern and interest of the therapist may often be interpreted as sexual interest by these clients, whereas these situations can be avoided if the therapist is a woman. Rawlings and Carter assert that the roles of lover and therapist should never be confused and that sexual involvement with a client is indefensible. Sexual feelings during the process of psychotherapy should be dealt with verbally rather than acted out, since the message conveyed to the woman client through sexual involvement with her male therapist is that somehow her sexual responsiveness is the most important prerequisite for her emotional adjustment.

5. It would be preferable for men not to treat women during the process of a divorce. As we discussed in Chapter 6, many women and men go through stages of grief following the death of the marital relationship. Women, because of their strong sense of identity with the lost wife role, are often tremendously vulnerable to intense feelings of dependency and insecurity which they may try to transfer to their male therapists instead of moving ahead psychologically

toward autonomy. According to Rawlings and Carter, when their fantasies about their therapist are not realized, these recently divorced women often begin looking for another man to replace the therapist instead of learning anything or growing as a person from the therapy experience.

Rawlings and Carter are specifically concerned with the process of psychotherapy for women, and they do not go on to list some of the possible situations in which women should not treat men. However, it seems reasonable to assume that for several of the situations they mention a woman might be less effective than a man with a male client. For example, it may be that a woman would be less effective than a man as a therapist with an all-male group, and a woman with "rescue fantasies" about men may not be the best person to counsel a man who is struggling with an unhappy marriage. Similarly, female therapists might be advised not to do therapy with men who are hostile toward women until the client has worked through some of his hostility with a male therapist, and female therapists should also avoid becoming sexually involved with their clients. As Stricker (1977) points out, the issue of sexual relationships between therapists and clients almost always involves male therapists and female clients since the vast majority of therapists are male and the majority of patients are female. Nevertheless, he, like Rawlings and Carter, maintains that sexual relations between any therapist and any patient are always inappropriate, exploitative, and unethical, and they can often be destructive.

Sexual contact during psychotherapy does occur and not all mental-health professionals agree that this behavior is unethical or damaging to the clients. Kardener et al. (1973) surveyed the attitudes of male physicians and psychiatrists and found that approximately 5 percent acknowledged having had sexual intercourse with their patients, and 20 percent indicated that there were situations when such activity might be beneficial. Similarly, Sherman et al. (1978) found that when their sample of male and female psychologists, social workers, and psychiatrists was asked about sexual intimacy between therapists and clients, 6 percent of these mental-health professionals indicated that they were either neutral or felt that there were occasions when sexual intimacy could be helpful. Apparently, a small minority of therapists believe there are no ethical problems concerning sexual relations with their clients in spite of the indications to the contrary.

Countertransference

Related to the issue of sexual contact with patients is countertransference, or the attitudes and feelings that the therapist has toward a particular client. In psychoanalytic theory, countertransference has been defined as the therapist's own conscious and unconscious conflicts which may affect his or her understanding and therapeutic effectiveness. For this discussion, however, we will refer to the term in a broader sense to include any perceptions and experiences of the therapists that subsequently affect their experiences with their clients.

Saretsky (1977) has stated that although *ideally* a therapist should remain a nonjudgmental participant who does not impose personal attitudes and values upon a client, *realistically* the therapist is a product of the same environment as the client and has been exposed to similar values and attitudes. She maintains that all mental-health professionals are susceptible to a loss of balanced therapeutic objectivity in certain situations and describes herself as being especially vulnerable as a result of her "relatively new-found feminist orientation." She relates that it sometimes takes restraint on her part not to strive to transform her female clients into people that they sometimes have no desire to be or before they are capable of making such changes. Eisenbud (1977) asserts that in the countertransference of female therapists today there is often a drive for "common cause" with other women, and feels that her own needs to relate to other women are very strong. According to Hare-

Mustin (1977), even therapists are made to feel uneasy when people behave in unexpected ways, and there is evidence that passive men and aggressive women make male therapists anxious, whereas female therapists have been found to be most bothered by excesses in stereotypes, such as the "macho" man or the "super-feminine" woman.

Abramowitz et al. (1976) investigated sex-role-related countertransference in psychotherapy and found that sex roles appear to have an effect on the ways therapists treat their clients. According to these investigators, male therapists tend to see their female clients for a greater number of psychotherapy sessions than their male clients, whereas there is no association between the sex of the clients and the number of sessions for female therapists. There is, however, a tendency for women to see older and less well-educated men for more sessions than younger and more highly educated men. There is also a tendency for women to treat other women rather than see men, and to treat proportionally fewer single or divorced men as compared to married men. Abramowitz et al. speculate that male therapists may extend their contact with women because of their own sexual curiosity and their voyeuristic needs. Similarly, men may limit their contact with other men because of the socialized competition between men. For example, the therapist may have a need to demonstrate his competence by "curing" the male client quickly, or the male client's inability to cope may be particularly threatening to the male therapist. The investigators suggest that women who avoid men as patients may be avoiding having to deal with the feelings activated during therapy by a socially attractive male patient, especially if he is young, well-educated, and sexually "uncommited."

Brodsky (1977) discusses the issue of countertransference from a training viewpoint and maintains that the feelings, attitudes, and personal interactions that occur between supervisor and therapy student and between therapy student and client have important implications for the personal and professional growth of all three people involved. She contends that the sex of the participants has a significant effect on the overall training experience as well as on the quality of the current and future service to clients. Brodsky suggests that there are four traits which can particularly affect sex-related countertransference issues: power, nurturance, empathy, and seduction. She maintains that it is important for both male and female student therapists to be supervised by both male and female professionals and for students of both sexes to be assigned to both male and female clients. Female supervisors must realize, as Brodsky herself admits learning, that male students will not reject their supervision, but will often be grateful for the assistance provided and show admiration or respect for the supervision. In addition, male supervisors must learn to be aware of the sex-role consequences of the authoritive man and dependent woman trainee relationship, since therapist growth can be damaged if the supervisor and trainee exaggerate the powerlessness of the female trainee. Similarly, both male and female supervisors must become aware of their own needs to provide or reject nurturance and empathy. For example, in some instances a female supervisor might try to reject her feelings of nurturance or empathy in order to appear more competent and powerful, whereas a male supervisor may be too protective, especially of his female trainees, and may actually be encouraging incompetence and dependency rather than fostering confidence and independence. Brodsky further suggests that both supervisors and therapy trainees must deal with their own sexual feelings toward each other as well as toward clients. All trainees should be assigned men and women as clients and should be encouraged to discuss and understand their positive and negative reactions to these various clients. Similarly, supervisors and trainees must be aware of the sexual implications of their various roles and learn to confront and deal with seductive behavior toward or from clients as well as toward or from each other in the supervisor/trainee relationship.

Implications for Mental-Health Professionals

One of the most important implications of our discussion of psychotherapy is the apparent lack of knowledge and information about relevant issues on the part of many mental-health professionals. It's impossible to provide relevant and appropriate services to clients if you are ignorant of the current literature and research in the mental-health field. For example, if you still believe that men and women are only mentally healthy when they are acting out their "appropriate" sex roles, you are doing many of your clients a disservice by encouraging them to accept what are now recognized as unhealthy roles for many women and men. Similarly, if you are treating your male and female clients differently and assuming that most women you see are emotionally disturbed whereas most men have situational problems that are usually related to occupational stress, you are reinforcing existing stereotypes without really considering the implications of your actions. Think about your own behavior as a therapist or counselor. Chances are you see more women than men as clients, and you probably feel you are providing helpful services to most of these women. On the other hand, are you aware of most of the current issues pertinent to women; for example, that marriage tends to have a more negative effect on women than on men, or that most women do not suffer severe psychological trauma after an abortion, or that most of the drug prescriptions written in this country are intended for women instead of men?

Although many people have expressed opinions as to whether men or women should provide psychotherapy services for women, there has been much less discussion about the potential effects of male and female therapists on male clients. It seems reasonable to assume that if male and female therapists treat women differently, they would also treat men differently, and at least for some men, a female therapist might be more helpful. However, at the present time, the accumulated research evidence is somewhat contradictory, and it appears that the sex of the therapist alone is not as important as his or her theoretical orientation and model of mental health. While sex of the therapist and sex of the client may make a difference in individual cases, both men and women can be sexist in their approach to psychotherapy and both can be nonsexist. The distinction between bad therapy and sexist therapy is also an important one since incompetent therapists are dangerous to all clients, whereas sexist therapy is mainly damaging to women.

Biases in any direction are undesirable in psychotherapy and women therapists, especially, may have to guard against substituting new biases for old ones and trying to fit all female clients into a more liberated sex role. It is just as undesirable to condemn a woman for being satisfied in her role as wife and mother as it is to limit the career opportunities for women. Similarly, some men may not be ready to give up their macho sex roles even though you as a therapist feel they are limiting their own life-styles and may be literally shortening their own life spans by repressing their emotions and accepting all of the responsibility and stress for their careers and the maintenance of their families.

As a mental-health professional you also need to be aware that your responsibility to your clients doesn't end once you have helped them break out of confining sex roles or work through a major crisis in their lives. You also need to help your clients deal with the consequences of their decisions and their actions. For example, a woman who decides to leave her husband and establish a career will need help and support not only while she is struggling with the decision, but after she has made it in order that she can deal with the pressures from within herself as well as from society. Similarly, a man who is unhappy with his marriage and his profession may make the decision while in therapy to change his situation in one or the other or both roles, and it is after he makes his decision that he will need the most help in dealing with the anxiety, guilt, and self-doubt that result from placing himself in a vulnerable position within society.

The issue of countertransference is also relevant for all mental-health professionals since all therapists bring their own values and experiences into the therapy sessions. Think about the clients who make you the most uncomfortable as a therapist. Are they older or younger than you? Are they men or women? What kinds of problems do they have that make you uncomfortable? Are you aware of experiences in your own life that might make you an ineffective therapist with certain clients? If you don't like a client or feel uncomfortable with a client because he or she triggers negative or anxious feelings inside you, think about how you handle the situation. Would you continue therapy or refer the client to another therapist? As an example of countertransference, imagine yourself as a therapist with an attractive client who is a woman if you are a man or who is a man if you are a woman. You have been seeing this client for several sessions and you are aware that you like the client and the client likes you, and the therapy appears to be progressing well. During one of the sessions the client confesses that he or she is in love with you and has been fantasizing about having a sexual relationship with you. What are your feelings and your reactions? Think about how you would handle the situation. There is some evidence that men in this position fear both rejecting the client and seducing the client; that is, they feel if they seem pleased or reassure the client she will misinterpret these actions as a sexual invitation, whereas if they don't respond positively she will feel rejected. Female therapists, on the other hand, are often more concerned about their own safety; that is, that the client might try to sexually attack them or try to pursue the relationship outside of therapy (Brodsky, 1977). How do your reactions match with these of other therapists and therapists in training?

Now imagine yourself with a same-sex client that you like and who likes you and who also announces that he or she is in love with you and fantasizes having sexual contact with you. Now what are your feelings and your reactions? Think about how you might handle this situation differently and whether or not you would feel more or less threatened by this client. Probably you feel more uncomfortable in this situation if you are a man, since many men tend to react very negatively to other men who do not follow prescribed sex roles. If you are a woman you probably also feel uncomfortable, but you may not be as fearful for your own safety as you were with the male client, and you may be able to be more accepting of this client's behavior than a male therapist in the same situation. What is most important is that you realize that you do respond differently to different clients and that you may not be as effective a therapist with one client as with another. Sometimes it is appropriate to refer particular clients to another therapist, especially when these clients trigger conflict areas in you that lessen your ability to help provide helpful services.

Nonsexist and Feminist Psychotherapy

We have discussed the potentially damaging effects of incompetent and sexist therapy, and we have examined the advantages of therapy that is relatively free from the biases of stereotyped sex roles. It now seems appropriate that we turn our attention to a discussion of the concepts of nonsexist and feminist psychotherapy. Nonsexist and feminist therapies are similar in that almost all existing therapeutic techniques can be used as long as the therapists themselves treat men and women equally and allow their clients to determine their own life-styles without the constrictions of stereotyped sex roles. Therapists may be either men or women, and even the term "feminist" includes both women and men. Williams (1976) defines a feminist therapist as a person who believes that it is healthy rather than neurotic for women to explore alternative ways of living. Such a therapist also defines healthy women as those who support themselves economically and enjoy their work and the sense of competence they have as a result of their productivity. Similarly, healthy women see other women as well as men as sources of friendship and love, and they do not feel that they are required to care for or provide services for other people except as a genuine expression of their love for them.

Although the concepts of feminist and nonsexist therapy have often been used interchangeably, Rawlings and Carter (1977) make several distinctions between the two. The major distinction they make is that feminist psychotherapy incorporates the philosophy and the political values of the women's movement, whereas nonsexist therapy does not. Therefore, feminist therapy may be more appropriate for some clients than for others; for example, it might be very appropriate for an independent woman who is aware of sex-role issues and is dissatisfied with her present life status, whereas it might be less appropriate than nonsexist therapy for a woman who is dependent and passive and is not yet aware of alternatives to her present stereotyped sex role. According to Rawlings and Carter, nonsexist therapy and feminist therapy are based on similar but not identical assumptions and strategies.

Nonsexist therapy is based on the assumptions that: (1) The therapist is aware of his or her own values and has learned what the sexist issues are. (2) There are no prescribed sex-role behaviors, and clients are encouraged to make decisions about their own behavior based on what they want instead of on what is expected of them by others. (3) Sex-role reversals in life-style are not labeled pathological, and if a woman wants to be assertive and independent and a man wants to be a househusband, the therapist will let the client choose for herself or himself. (4) Marriage is not regarded as any better an outcome of therapy for a woman or a man. (5) Both men and women are encouraged to be androgynous and flexible in their sex roles. (6) Theories based on differences in anatomy are rejected.

The assumptions underlying feminist therapy include: (1) Women have inferior status because they have less political and economic power than men. (2) The primary source of psychopathology for women is social, not personal. (3) Feminist therapy is opposed to personal adjustment to social conditions, and the goals of therapy are social and political change. (4) Other women are not the enemy, and men are not the enemy either. (5) Women must be economically and psychologically independent. (6) Relationships of love, friendship, and marriage should be equal in personal power. (7) Major differences between "appropriate" sex-role behavior for the two sexes must disappear in order to eliminate sex-role expectations and stereotyping.

It is apparent from these descriptions of the basic assumptions of feminist and nonsexist therapy that both approaches emphasize an androgynous model of mental health, and both reject anatomy and biology as explanations for the differences in behavior of women and men. Furthermore, both approaches emphasize the importance of the therapist's own awareness of sex-role issues and the negative effects of stereotyping. According to Rawlings and Carter, these two types of therapy are less similar in regard to the specific strategies they recommend. For example, the three main strategies of nonsexist therapy are fairly general and include: (1) The therapist does not use the power of his or her position to reinforce or punish "appropriate" or "inappropriate" sex-role behavior. (2) Diagnoses are not based on deviations from prescribed sex-role behavior. (3) Sex-biased tests are not used. On the other hand, the strategies of feminist psychotherapy are more specific and include several strategies: (1) The values of the therapists regarding women's roles must be made known to the client before therapy begins. (2) The therapist and the client enter into a contract specifying the behavior that the client wants to change. (3) The therapist provides direct and indirect instruction and teaches the client various kinds of relevant behavior and provides books and references to help the client "be her own therapist." (4) Feminist therapy is done most effectively in groups. (5) Engaging in social action is an essential part of therapy.

Rawlings and Carter maintain that while many therapists may qualify as nonsexist therapists, they should not call themselves feminist therapists if they are not feminists. Having a professional degree and believing that women and men should be equal are not sufficient qualifications to enable a therapist to provide feminist therapy, since feminist therapy requires that the therapist himself or herself be politically and socially active and be familiar with the literature concerning feminist issues. Therefore, most mental-health professionals will find it easier and perhaps more in line with their own feelings and values to provide nonsexist therapy rather than feminist therapy for their clients, especially since nonsexist strategies apply equally well to both women and men. The New York Chapter of NOW (1978) has published a consumer's guide to nonsexist therapy that describes the process of nonsexist therapy and provides guidelines to help potential clients choose a nonsexist therapist. This booklet may also be useful for mental-health professionals who are interested in nonsexist therapy, since it includes a list of the rights of clients in therapy as well as a description of the requirements for a nonsexist therapeutic relationship.

Assertion Training

In addition to providing nonsexist therapy for their clients, an increasing number of therapists are supplementing therapy with specific types of training to counteract deficiencies in socialization skills due to the effects of sex-role stereotyping. The most widely used of these types of supplemental training are assertion training and consciousness raising.

According to Jakubowski (1977), assertion involves standing up for your interpersonal rights without violating the rights of another person during the process, and nonassertion is failing to stand up for your rights and consequently permitting your rights to be violated by other people. In other words, being assertive means expressing your values and feelings directly and appropriately rather than failing to say what you really mean or expressing yourself in a self-conscious, ineffective manner. Being assertive does not mean the same thing as being aggressive, however, since aggression involves attempting to dominate or humiliate other people. In our society, most men are socialized to be assertive and are reinforced for assertive behavior, whereas most women are reinforced for being nonassertive. Assertion training can be beneficial for both women and men who have difficulty standing up for their rights as individuals, but as a result of our sex-role stereotyping, more women than men find it difficult to be assertive.

According to Jakubowski, there are several possible factors that can prevent people from acting assertively. They may not believe they have the right to be assertive, or they may have had experiences that have caused them to be afraid to be assertive. Another possibility is that some people may never have learned the necessary skills to become assertive. Regardless of the cause, however, nonassertive people generally have little self-confidence or self-esteem, and their needs and opinions are usually disregarded by other people. When nonassertive people try to get their needs satisfied, they may resort to using forms of manipulation such as crying or trying to act in ways to please other people in order to get what they want instead of directly expressing their desires. They may also use forms of indirect aggression such as backbiting or complaining to other people instead of standing up for themselves. After a long period of failing to act assertively, people may accumulate hurt and angry feelings until they finally explode in aggressive anger. Although they may feel better temporarily, they often feel guilty and disgusted with themselves later, and the recipient of their anger typically feels angry and vengeful.

A major goal of assertion training is to help clients develop a personal belief system that will help them support and justify their acting assertively. According to Jakubowski (1977, 1978), it is important that, in addition to believing that they have certain rights which they are entitled to exercise, clients learn to believe that they will be happier if they assert their rights and that nonassertion is harmful in the long run. For example, clients need to understand that not being assertive will eventually hurt interpersonal relationships since it prevents people from sharing genuine thoughts and feelings and getting to know each other as they really are.

Jakubowski maintains that the most effective assertion training occurs in same-sex groups of six to ten people with a same-sex therapist who can serve as a role model for the group. She has suggested a four-phase assertion training program which includes the following phases: (1) helping clients to distinguish among assertive, aggressive, and nonassertive behavior and motivating clients to become more assertive; (2) helping clients develop a belief system to support their assertive behavior; (3) removing psychological obstacles that prevent clients from using assertive skills, such as the fear that expressing anger will destroy relationships; and (4) developing assertive skills through active practice methods.

In order to facilitate assertion training, Jakubowski recommends a variety of techniques. One of these techniques is an assertive-discrimination exercise in which clients listen to a series of tape-recorded statements and try to decide whether the statements are assertive, aggressive, or nonassertive. For example, you might listen to a situation in which an acquaintance has asked to borrow your car for an evening, and you would then hear various possible responses to this request, such as "Are you crazy! I don't lend my car to anyone!" (aggressive), or "I don't know—well it's not worth getting into a fuss about, you can borrow it" (nonassertive), or "I'd really like to help you out, but I don't feel comfortable about loaning my car" (assertive). A second technique involves the use of "probes" to help clients think about developing a more assertive belief system. For example, the therapist might say to the client, "Tell me why you permit others to have these rights (to be assertive) but you deny them for yourself," or "What caused you to believe that you don't have these rights?" Another technique recommended by Jakubowski involves the use of behavioral rehearsal or role playing to help the client practice and rehearse specific assertive responses in order to learn the skills necessary for assertive behavior. Jakubowski cautions that clients often pass through an aggressive phase in the course of assertion training and that they may also do a certain amount of "assertion for the sake of assertion" rather than having a more natural style of assertiveness which they can choose to exercise if they wish. She maintains that this behavior usually ceases by the end of training when the clients are more self-confident and skillful in their use of assertion skills.

Consciousness-Raising (CR) Groups

Another supplement or alternative to psychotherapy is the use of consciousness-raising groups. CR is not therapy in the usual sense, since the settings are quite different and the groups are leaderless. The CR groups typically consist of a small group of same-sex participants, usually women, who meet in each others' homes to talk about sex-role issues and share personal experiences. Participants are supportive of each other, but usually do not give specific advice or criticize each other. Fish (1975) analyzed the content of the conversation during several sessions of a women's CR group and found four main content categories, including (1) feelings about other women; (2) self-perception, or how the women feel about themselves; (3) feelings about men; and (4) feelings about motherhood and children.

Williams (1977) maintains that for many women, CR groups provide their first opportunities for relating in a trusting and noncompetitive way with other women, and consequently, the feeling of a common bond of sisterhood often becomes very strong in these groups. Furthermore, Brodsky (1977) feels that CR groups can be more effective than therapy groups in helping women with identity problems, because the group allows women to work out their identity with other women without the dominance-submission interaction patterns that tend to emerge when men are present. Also, it is assumed that the environment is the cause of women's problems, and the discussion is topic-oriented rather than encouraging self-disclosure and a search for individual corrective emotional experiences. Nevertheless, Brodsky does not feel that CR groups are suitable for all women, especially if they are in need of intensive psychotherapy and are too defensive or too vulnerable to benefit from the group process. Also, as Williams (1977) notes, CR groups are mainly beneficial for middle-class, educated women who are psychologically well-adjusted and who need help breaking out of old patterns of guilt and self-destructiveness. Brodsky further maintains that participating in or studying CR groups is one way to learn about alternatives to sexism in psychotherapy. Even though not all therapists can or want to be feminist therapists, all should aspire to be nonsexist therapists. Psychotherapy is "good" when it is appropriate for the person needing help, and psychotherapy cannot be good for men or women if it is based on sexist beliefs.

In this chapter, we have discussed the process of psychotherapy for men and women and have examined some of the relevant issues and implications pertaining to psychotherapy. We have also looked at the differences between feminist and nonsexist therapy and have discussed the two major supplementary techniques, assertion training and consciousness-raising groups. In the next chapter, we will look at some of the implications of sex-role issues and nonsexist techniques for training programs and for providing services for various client populations within our society.

8

Sex Roles and Social Issues

Race and Social Class

Almost all of the research and literature pertaining to the development of sex roles and stereotypes are based on white middle-class American women and men. Other groups within our society, including men and women who are nonwhite or in the lower socioeconomic class, have not been as thoroughly investigated, and it is not at all clear how appropriate the available research results are for these other groups.

There are obvious parallels between the struggles against racial biases and sexual biases in the United States. Both women and blacks have faced discrimination and stereotyping, which have limited or prevented fulfillment of their potentialities. Both groups have often been assumed to be biologically inferior when compared to the dominant groups in society, and both groups have often been expected and encouraged to pursue low-status life roles. Similarly, discriminatory practices against both blacks and women have been apparent in education and employment. At the same time, however, sex roles for black women and men apparently differ in important ways from those expected of white women and men. For example, the traditional roles of full-time housewife and mother are usually not appropriate for the black woman, who, because of economic necessity, must often assume the multiple roles of housewife, mother, head of household, and wage earner. Black women in America have always been relatively more independent of black men than have white women of white men; and black women, unlike white women, have a history of combining outside employment and motherhood. Raising children is still a major sex role for black women, but they also are socialized from an early age to anticipate the worker role.

Sex-role development and socialization for black girls and boys begins in the home, but their homes are usually quite different from those of middle-class white girls and boys. The black child is more likely to live with a single parent, and from an early age may be cared for by other relatives or neighbors. Consequently, although the mother has a strong influence on the adult expectations of the black child, socializing agents other than the parents are likely to influence development. Peer groups and various adult relatives and acquaintances take on more role-model significance at an earlier age for black children than for white children. Research evidence also suggests that black girls are socialized to become more independent, more autonomous, and stronger than white girls and that black girls tend to identify with the image of the "strong black woman" rather than with the stereotype of the passive, dependent woman (Ladner, 1971). Black girls apparently assume the adult female role much earlier than white girls, and they learn to relate to boys sexually at an earlier age (Broderick, 1965). Silverstein and Krate (1975) found that black children living in Harlem became self-reliant and independent at an early age in order to survive.

In contrast to expectations for white children, educational and occupational aspirations are accepted and encouraged for black girls, and working is regarded as an appropriate female role. Black mothers tend to have even higher educational aspirations for their daughters than for their sons, and in intact black families, there are no differences in aspirations for boys and girls as there are in white families (Ladner, 1971). Young black girls are encouraged to rely on their own achievements, and they are not encouraged to rely on men and marriage for future security.

The disproportionate sex ratio in the black population is more dramatic than in any other group in the United States. Within the white population an excess of women appears in middle age or later, whereas in the black population the imbalance is present from age fourteen. In 1970 there were approximately 91 black men to 100 black women, and the ratio appears to be decreasing (Malina, 1973). The male death rate is higher, and the life expectancy for males is shorter than that of females for all races. The survival of the black male is further threatened by the conditions of poverty, crowding, poor health-care facilities, and minimal protection against accidents and violence that often prevail in the black environment. Consequently, there are not enough men available for all black women, and black women cannot usually expect to be economically dependent upon black males. Furthermore, Epstein (1973) found that even when black women do marry and even when their black husbands are college-educated men, these women still cannot consider totally withdrawing from the work world, since the black man's education does not necessarily guarantee financial security and success.

Black women have often carried a disproportionate share of responsibility for the black family, and the female head of household is more prevalent in black than in white society. Because there are fewer men in the black society and because both black women and black men must work in order to survive economically, the black community utilizes the resources of all of its members, and in general, there are more egalitarian relationships between black men and women than between white men and women. Research indicates that black men and women have very similar expectations about sex roles in marriage and childrearing and that both men and women prefer a balance of self-actualizing and family orientations for women (Steinmann and Fox, 1970). Scanzoni (1975) also found that black women and men tend to develop more egalitarian marital relationships than white women and men. Black women apparently enjoy higher status within their own community than white women do in theirs.

At the same time, however, the position of the black woman has often been described as one of dominance or matriarchy that overpowers and overshadows the role of the black man in the family and in the community. Because the dominant white society has often made it difficult for the black man to assume the economic role as head of the household, the earning power of the black woman has often placed her in what appears to be a powerful position. However, statistics indicate that nonwhite women have the lowest average wage of any group in our society; and nonwhite men, even though they earn less than white men, earn more money on the average than either white or nonwhite women. Therefore, this concentration of black women at the lowest level of the employment scale indicates that the favored economic position of the black woman in relation to the black man is a myth and that the extent of black matriarchy is probably exaggerated and misinterpreted (Jackson, 1973).

Black women without husbands do tend to function more efficiently than white women without husbands, and black mothers are better able to provide adequate role models for their sons when fathers are absent (Hartnagel, 1970). Nevertheless, even though black women are able to be both expressive and instrumental, whereas most white women have been socialized to be primarily expressive, this does not necessarily imply that black women dominate or emasculate black men. The stereotypes that define men as instrumental and dominant and women as expressive and dependent have traditionally been products of the white culture and have only relatively recently surfaced in the black community.

In the 1960s, many black male spokesmen for civil rights apparently hypothesized a connection between white supremacy and male dominance and encouraged sexism as a method of overcoming racism. Many black men appeared to believe that the restoration of the black man should take precedence over the development of the black woman. Consequently, black women often felt disloyal to racial interests if they insisted upon women's rights and wanted to participate in decision making and leadership positions within the black movement. Instead they were often encouraged to stay in the background and raise their children and support their men. In 1970, a "Black Declaration of Independence," signed by members of the National Committee of Black Churchmen, appeared in *The New York Times.* The document discussed the equality of all "men" and also contained a long list of black male "heroes" prominent in the struggle for liberation. The contributions of black women were ignored.

Although black women have tended to identify discrimination against them as primarily racial and consequently have usually given highest priority to the struggle for civil rights, they have had to adjust to the double burden of discrimination based upon both race and sex. Black and white women share the common burden of sex discrimination, but the black woman must somehow combine the needs to develop as a person and to retain her status as an equal to the black man, while at the same time supporting and aiding the black movement. Faced with these dual barriers, black women have often found sex bias to be at least as formidable as racial bias.

When the positions of white women and black women are compared, the results indicate that the black woman remains single more often than the white woman, bears more children, is in the labor market longer, has less education, is widowed earlier, and often carries a heavier economic responsibility than the white woman (Murray, 1970). Even in light of these differences, black women have apparently endured with dignity, strength, and courage. They appear to have developed adaptive psychological resources to deal with their situations and to have immense strengths and coping abilities.

One would expect blacks to report low self-esteem as a consequence of the negative views of them held by the dominant white culture. However, this has not been apparent in the results of most of the research on black women and black men (Ladner, 1971; Rosenberg, 1972; Guterman, 1972). The results of earlier studies that indicated that blacks have negative self-concepts may no longer apply to contemporary black women and men who are apparently no longer as concerned about shades of skin color and white standards of beauty as their older brothers and sisters were. Even though they are often discriminated against both racially and sexually, black women, especially, tend to be resilient and capable of coping (Epstein, 1973).

In some ways, black women seem to have advantages over white women. They have been accepted as valuable members of their black society, and within that society they have often had equal rights with black men. Their sex-role socialization has generally been more comprehensive than sex-role socialization for white women and has included both a family orientation and an employment orientation. Consequently, black women seem more prepared than white women to take advantage of some of the opportunities arising for women. At the same time, however, the powerful white society often considers black women as inferior to white women and socially, politically, and economically, often excludes black women from its definition of womanhood and femininity. Whenever black women compete for a position or status generally identified with white women they are often intimidated or ignored.

King (1973) has referred to the black women as America's "other woman." According to King, in America there is a kind of nonrecognition of the black woman's existence that discourages any serious consideration of her unique problems. Since white women are apparently no less racist than white men, King concludes that it would be naive to discount the influence that racism will have on decision making in the women's movement. Yet, because of their traditions of independence and their long experience in civil rights, black women may be equipped better than most white women to assume leadership roles within the growing movement for women's rights. Black and white women are usually not separated by the power relationships that separate and antagonize black and white men, and therefore, productive communication and cooperation seem possible and necessary.

Implications for Mental-Health Professionals

Sex roles for most black women and men apparently differ in important ways from those expected of white, middle-class women and men. Therefore, when providing services for black clients, mental-health professionals need to be aware of any stereotyped expectations they may have about these clients, whether these expectations are based on race and/or sex variables. Ford (1978) maintains that often counselors assume that black clients are functioning within the lowest social positions in society and consequently must have the lowest self-esteem. She points out that black clients differ widely in social and economic status and, as we noted previously, often have higher levels of self-esteem than white clients. Ford also suggests that instead of trying to identify the weaknesses of black clients, counselors should reinforce the strengths of black clients and be supportive of their independence and self-reliance.

Even though more black women than white women are socialized to include employment as a part of their life plans, Turner (1972) has suggested that for black women, full-time employment expectations may imply a deep sense of responsibility more than an anticipation of personal fulfillment. She found that among college students, 54 percent of the black women expected to work full time, whereas only 15 percent of the white women had these expectations. She also found that even though these black women expected to have to work full time, they indicated they would prefer less work responsibility and had negative attitudes about their mothers' employment. Consequently, career counselors and other service providers should not automatically assume that because a woman is black she is necessarily happier about her sex-role requirements than a white woman. Although she expects to work, she may be realistically anticipating the prospects of low pay and low-status employment, and she may not feel that she will be able to find self-expression through her employment experiences.

Epstein (1973) points out, however, that although a black woman's sex and race are often evaluated negatively by society, for the competent and educated black woman these two attributes can often work positively in her career planning, since many organizations want to hire black women to meet federal regulations. She found that black professional women are also seen as more professionally serious than their white counterparts, and she suggests that counselors can assist black women in taking advantage of their "double-negative-equals-positive" position in the job market. At the same time, however, black women who are hired to "meet federal regulations" can be expected to face the same types of discrimination and problems as other "tokens" in the work world, as we discussed in Chapter 5.

Counselors working with black men also need to be aware of the different socialization process and expectations for black and white men as well as for black men and black women. For example, in a study comparing fear of success in black and white women and men, black men had higher fear of success than black women, whereas the reverse was found for white men and women (Horner, 1972).

Kirk (1975), in an attempt to help counselors understand the sex-role development of black clients, has suggested several developmental stages that can serve as a general guide. These stages include (1) Self-hate—At this stage, the clients are hostile and fearful. (2) Self-pity—The clients' behavior is usually self-indulgent, and they still view the world as evil and hostile. (3) Self-examination—The clients begin to explore their cultural heritage and to try out new roles and images. (4) Self-knowledge—The clients are more self-confident and assertive and are working toward the development of individual identities. (5) Self-esteem—The clients have realized their own identities and the dignity of their blackness. They feel they are useful and productive members of society.

Perhaps the major implication for mental-health professionals is indicated by the relative lack of research and literature pertaining to clients other than those who are white and middle-class. In order to provide services effectively to other groups within our society, we need more specific information about the values and needs of these men and women and their sex-role expectations and socialization processes. For a more comprehensive discussion of minority issues in mental health, refer to Smith et al. (1978).

Case Study Example

Donna M, a twenty-eight-year-old black graduate student in clinical psychology, makes an appointment to see you because you are her supervisor and advisor. She is divorced and has two children. Donna is in trouble academically in the psychology program; she received three C's in required courses and has not been granted an assistantship for the next semester. You have supervised Donna in her clinical work and feel she has the potential to be a good clinician. She works especially well with black children and adults, and her career goals include finishing her Ph.D. and then working with black clients in the community. Donna is one of two black students in the clinical-psychology program. She has completed three years in the program and appears to be bright and motivated but has had difficulty from the beginning with courses that require written examinations and papers. She was accepted into the program on the basis of her strong letters of reference even though her undergraduate grades were just above average and her Graduate Record Exam scores were slightly lower than those of the other accepted students.

Donna arrives for her appointment visibly upset. She begins by telling you that she went before the review board to try to have her assistantship reinstated but that her request was refused. She becomes very angry as she speaks and begins talking about racial prejudice and discrimination and her feeling that she has to be twice as competent as the other students to be treated with the same amount of respect.

You are aware of the fact that although Donna works part time, she does not earn enough money to enable her to attend graduate school without an assistantship. You have also been told by other students that Donna is having discipline problems with her son, although Donna has not confided in you herself and does not do so now.

Donna asks you to intervene on her behalf and to help her stay in the program. It is obvious that she likes and respects you, but when you ask her personal questions she gives evasive answers and indicates that "everything is fine" except for the "unfair" grades. You like her and respect her, but you find you are uncomfortable with her because there seems to be an invisible barrier that prevents you from understanding her as well as you feel you understand your other students.

Think about your reaction to Donna and her situation. She is a woman and she is black. She is also a graduate student in trouble academically. You are her closest role-model in the graduate program. What are your feelings? What might you be tempted to do? You could treat her like any other student and say, "a rule is a rule" and not go out on a limb for her, or you might make a special effort because she is *not* like the other students. Try to be aware of your feelings about her as a woman. Would you think a Ph.D. would be more or less important for her if she were a man? Try to be aware of your feelings about her as a black student. Would you have an easier time deciding what to do or would you make a different decision about her if she were white? How do you react to her anger and her accusations of racial discrimination? Do you feel guilty or angry or defensive or sorry for her? Do you think that your sex has anything to do with your feelings about Donna? Do you think you might feel differently if you were (weren't) black yourself?

After considering Donna's situation, many of you have probably discovered that you have different expectations for people on the basis of race as well as on the basis of sex and that it is often impossible to provide services for people without considering both of these variables.

Training and Reeducation

Throughout our discussion of sex roles and mental-health issues we have noted that bias is evident when clients are treated differently because of sex, race, age, or social class, and that clients have often received ineffective or limited services because of the biases held by professional-service providers. We are accumulating a large body of research data which is clarifying many of the problems with existing therapy techniques and testing materials for use with women and minority groups, and as more professionals become aware of these issues, biased expectations for clients based on sex roles are apparently changing. At the same time, however, these changing attitudes and expectations are often not being reflected in professional services. Consequently, it seems imperative that professional education programs and reeducation programs accept professional bias as a fact and strive to provide training programs that will remove these biases during future encounters with clients.

Schlossberg and Pietrofesa (1978) maintain that the first task is to convince mental-health professionals and educators that they, themselves, probably hold biases and that these biases affect their services to their clients and their effectiveness as supervisors and teachers. The second task is to integrate the facts about biases into training programs, and the third task is to begin developing materials for use in training programs to demonstrate the effects of biases. For example, they suggest the possible development of a self-administered instrument which might yield several bias scores or the development of role-playing situations that revolve around various types of possible biases.

Schlossberg and Pietrofesa have also suggested a training model that can be used to educate or reeducate mental-health professionals about their own value systems and sex-role biases. They propose a program that would include: (1) expanding the understanding of participants through lectures and reading; (2) raising the consciousness of participants regarding sexual bias through group techniques, such as small-group discussions or consciousness-raising groups; (3) promoting the acquisition of nonbiased helping skills through audio or video taping and role playing; and (4) fostering skill development in program planning and implementation through field practice and projects.

According to Schlossberg and Pietrofesa, the practicum experience probably provides one of the best opportunities for dealing with basic feelings and biases, since trainees can have supervised contacts with clients of different sexes, races, ages, and social classes and then receive feedback about their techniques and behavior. These authors also recommend the use of additional techniques such as the "fishbowl" technique where group participants are observed by other trainees and then receive feedback from the observers about their behavior, or the "helper-helpee" technique in which one trainee discusses a situation in his or her own life and another trainee attempts to provide a helping interaction. A group discussion would follow both of these techniques and would include the feelings of the participants as well as the feelings and evaluations of the observers and the supervisors.

Guzell (1977) maintains that women's studies courses should be made a required part of all training programs for mental-health professionals, and she makes a number of practical recommendations for the instructors of these courses. According to Guzell, timing in teaching is extremely important, and students should not be given an overload of potentially "explosive" material in too little time without opportunities to discuss and digest it. For example, both male and female students often react with strong emotions, such as anger, anxiety, or guilt, when they become aware of the effects of sex biases, and these feelings can lead to situations where women in the class begin verbally attacking men in the class and the men becoming angry and defensive themselves. Guzell suggests preparing the class ahead of time by discussing the potential emotions that these courses often evoke and avoiding excessive stereotyping of men as a backlash effect. Guzell also recommends establishing small discussion groups within the class in which relevant personal material can be shared and techniques such as role playing or assertion training can be incorporated into the course structure. She also recommends encouraging participants to share their feelings and experiences with significant others in their lives, such as husbands, wives, boyfriends, and girlfriends, and she strongly recommends stressing androgyny as a model of mental health.

Knefelkamp et al. (1978) maintain that training programs should be evaluated to determine whether they are fostering the development of relatively aware and unbiased professionals. They suggest asking the following questions of any training program: (1) Does the program foster only one "right" way of working with clients? (2) Does it allow a biased view of women and men to exist implicitly? (3) Does the training expose students to all types of clients? (4) Does the training foster a deep respect for individual differences? (5) Does it provide direction and support so that students can examine their own values, attitudes, and stereotyped beliefs? According to Knefelcamp et al., it is just as important for mental-health professionals to be aware of their own perceptions of sex-role issues as it is for them to recognize how their clients perceive themselves. Furthermore, the same type of self-examination that is necessary for students in training is every bit as necessary for practitioners already in the profession.

In addition to the recommendations and suggestions for training that we have just discussed, it seems appropriate and necessary to include the recommendation that more qualified women and minority-group members should be encouraged to enter training programs in the mental-health fields at the professional levels. Stereotypes need to be changed so that more women and blacks can begin focusing on professional careers as role possibilities early in their life cycles and can acquire the necessary skills and self-confidence for success in graduate training programs. If these people are trained to be nonsexist, nonbiased professionals, they will provide the best possible role models for other women and minority-group members aspiring to professional careers within the mental-health field.

Therapist Power

Competent, responsible, unbiased training programs produce competent, responsible, unbiased mental-health professionals who can go on to use their knowledge and their expertise to influence the attitudes and behavior of numerous people within our society. Therapists, counselors, and educators exert great influence upon individuals and groups and are usually regarded as powerful members of society. Even though there is disagreement within the mental-health field about whether this power should be used directly (for example, in behavior modification) or indirectly (for example, in nondirective counseling), most professionals would agree that they do influence if not manipulate the behavior of their clients.

Gillis (1974) maintains that all therapy and counseling orientations recommend and incorporate influencing techniques, and he has identified two major sources of therapist power: command power and friendship power. According to Gillis, command power is established by the therapy situation itself. Therapists often have impressive titles, such as "Dr." or "Professor," and even without these titles they are authority figures because of their positions. Usually therapists have their own offices with displays of impressive diplomas and certificates, and often an aura of power is suggested by such things as the office furnishings and the therapist's language usage and style of dress. Furthermore, the majority of therapists are men and the majority of clients are women, and most men have more power in our society than most women.

Friendship power means the same thing as establishing rapport with the client. Therapists present themselves as interested, educated, decent people and establish relationships with their clients that the clients want to maintain. Typically, clients value these relationships and seek the continued approval and support of their therapists, because they believe that the therapists care about them and can help them seek relief from their problems.

Frank (1961) uses the term "placebo effect" to account for therapist power. In medicine, a placebo is a "sugar pill," or a substance that has no medical effects but is sometimes used to increase the patients' expectation of cure. According to Frank, most clients enter into a therapy or counseling relationship with the expectation that they will be helped, and this positive expectation may have a more powerful influence on therapy outcome than any of the specific techniques used by the therapist. Similarly, Rawlings and Carter (1977) point out that often the sheer inconvenience of beginning and continuing in psychotherapy is inconsistent with attitudes that therapy is not very useful. For example, "initiation" into therapy may include taking stressful psychological tests, being placed on a long waiting list, paying high fees, and driving long distances for the therapy sessions. They suggest that the harder it is to find a therapist and to continue therapy, the more clients are apt to feel that therapy and therapists are worthwhile and necessary.

Regardless of the specific reasons, mental-health professionals are powerful members of our society, and because of their power they are in positions to influence the attitudes and behavior of other people within our society. Mental-health professionals can be effective socially and politically to change existing sex roles and to encourage nonsexist, nonbiased expectations and opportunities for all people. In order to be effective, however, educators, therapists, and counselors must first acknowledge their own positions of influence and responsibility within their communities and become aware of their own biased attitudes and value systems. Only then will they be able to provide nonbiased services to their clients and society.

View of the Future

Throughout our discussion of sex-role issues, we have noted many areas in which changes are slowly beginning to occur as more and more people become aware of the negative effects of stereotyping on both women and men. For the future we might optimistically predict that role differences based on sex will be eliminated and an androgynous model of mental health will prevail, providing both men and women more freedom and flexibility in their lives. Men and women will have the same educational and career opportunities, and both will have more options in career and family combinations. Role sharing will replace sex-role requirements, and both parents will assume equal responsibility for their children. The father's role will be recognized as essential as the mother's role, and either (or both) parent may choose to work full time or part time. It will no longer be assumed that marriage is a necessary requirement for mental health for either women or men, and a greater variety of life-styles will be available for all people. In addition, you, as mental-health-service providers, will be aware of these changes as they are occurring and will be influencing and reinforcing healthy, nonsexist, unbiased attitudes and behavior within our society.

Bibliography

Abramowitz, C., and P. Dokecki (1977). The politics of clinical judgment: Early empirical returns. *Psychological Bulletin* 84:460–476.

Abramowitz, S., and C. Abramowitz (1973). Should prospective women clients seek out women practitioners? Intimations of a "ding-bat" effect in clinical evaluation. *Proceedings of the 81st Annual Convention of the American Psychological Association* 8:503.

Abramowitz, S., C. Abramowitz, C. Jackson, and B. Gomes (1973). The politics of clinical judgment: What nonliberal examiners infer about women who don't stifle themselves. *Journal of Consulting and Clinical Psychology* 41:385–391.

Abramowitz, S., C. Abramowitz, H. Roback, R. Corney, and E. McKee (1976). Sex-role related countertransference in psychotherapy. *Archives of General Psychiatry* 33:71–73.

Abramowitz, S., C. Abramowitz, H. Roback, and E. McKee (1974). Sex-role related countertransference in psychotherapy. Unpublished manuscript, Vanderbilt University, 1974.

Abramowitz, S., L. Weitz, J. Schwartz, S. Amira, B. Gomes, and C. Abramowitz (1975). Comparative counselor inferences toward women with medical school aspirations. *Journal of College Student Personnel* 16: 128–130.

Alper, T. (1973). The relationship between role orientations and achievement motivation in college women. *Journal of Personality* 41:9–31.

______ (1974). Achievement motivation in college women: A now-you-see-it-now-you-don't phenomenon. *American Psychologist* 29:194–203.

Alper, T., and E. Greenberger (1967). Relationship of picture structure to achievement motivation in college women. *Journal of Personality and Social Psychology* 7:362–371.

Alsbrook, L. (1976). Marital communication and sexism. *Social Casework* 57(8): 517–522.

American College Testing Program (1971). *Career Planning Program Brochure.* Iowa City, Iowa.

American Psychological Association (1975). Report of the Task Force on Sex Bias and Sex-Role Stereotyping in Psychotherapeutic Practice. *American Psychologist* 30:1169–1175.

Araji, S. (1977). Husbands' and wives' attitude-behavior congruence on family roles. *Journal of Marriage and the Family* (May): 309–320.

Aslin, A. (1978). Counseling "single-again" (divorced and widowed) women. In L. Harmon, J. Birk, L. Fitzgerald, and M. Tanny (eds.), *Counseling Women.* Monterey: Brooks/Cole, 230–240.

Astin, H. (1969). *The Woman Doctorate in America.* New York: Russell Sage.

______ (1973). Preparing women for careers in science and technology. Paper presented at the MIT Workshop on Women in Science and Technology, Boston, May.

Atkinson, J., and N. Feather (eds.) (1966). *A Theory of Achievement Motivation.* New York: Wiley.

Atkinson, J., and J. Raynor (eds.) (1974). *Motivation and Achievement.* Washington, D.C.: Winston and Sons.

Bandura, A., D. Ross, and S. Ross (1963). Imitation of film-mediated aggressive models. *Journal of Abnormal and Social Psychology* 66:3–11.

Barrett, C., P. Berg, E. Eaton, and F. Pomeroy (1974). Implications of women's liberation and the future of psychotherapy. *Psychotherapy: Theory, Research and Practice* 11:11–15.

Bart, P. (1971). The myth of value-free psychotherapy. In W. Bell and J. Mau (eds.), *The Sociology of the Future.* New York: Russell Sage Foundation, 113–159.

Baruch, G. (1972). Maternal influences upon college women's attitudes toward women and work. *Developmental Psychology* 6:32–37.

Baumrind, D. (1972). From each according to her ability. *School Review* 80:161–197.

Bem, S. (1972). Where have all the androgynous people gone? Paper presented at UCLA Symposium on Women, May.

______ (1974). The measurement of psychological androgyny. *Journal of Consulting and Clinical Psychology* 42(2): 155–162.

______ (1975). Sex-role adaptability: One consequence of psychological androgyny. *Journal of Personality and Social Psychology* 31(4): 634–643.

______ (1976). Probing the promise of androgyny. In A. Kaplan and J. Bean (eds.), *Beyond Sex-Role Stereotypes: Readings Toward a Psychology of Androgyny.* Boston: Little, Brown, 48–62.

Bem, S., and D. Bem (1976). Training the woman to know her place: The power of a nonconscious ideology. In S. Cox (ed.), *Female Psychology: The Emerging Self.* Chicago: SRA, 180–191.

Bernard, J. (1964). The adjustment of married mates. In H. Christensen (ed.), *Handbook of Marriage and the Family.* Skokie, Ill.: Rand McNally.

______ (1972). *The Future of Marriage.* New York: Bantam Books.

______ (1973). Adjusting the lives of women to the establishment. In C. Stoll, (ed.), *Sexism: Scientific Debates.* Reading, Mass.: Addison-Wesley.

Bianchini, J. (1976). Achievement tests and differentiated norms. Paper presented at the U.S. Office of Education Invitational Conference on Achievement Testing of Disadvantaged and Minority Students, May, Reston, Va.

Bingham, W., and E. House (1973). Counselors view women and work: Accuracy of information. *The Vocational Guidance Quarterly* (January): 262–268.

Birnbaum, J. (1975). Life patterns and self-esteem in gifted family-oriented and career-committed women. In M. Mednick, S. Tangri, and L. Hoffman (eds.), *Women and Achievement: Social and Motivational Analyses.* New York: Halsted Press, 396–419.

Block, J. H., J. Block, and D. Harrington (1974). The relationship of parental teaching strategies to ego-resiliency in preschool children. Paper presented at the Western Psychological Association meeting, San Francisco.

Block, J., A. von der Lippe, and J. H. Block (1973). Sex role and socialization patterns: Some personality concomitants and environmental antecedents. *Journal of Consulting and Clinical Psychology* 41:321–341.

Blood, R., and D. Wolfe (1960). *Husbands and Wives.* New York: Free Press.

Bodine, A. (1975). Sex differentiation in language. In B. Thorne and N. Henley (eds.), *Language and Sex: Difference and Dominance.* Rowley, Mass.: Newbury House, 130–151.

Bohannan, P. (ed.) (1970). *Divorce and After.* New York: Doubleday.

Broderick, C. (1965). Social heterosexual development among urban negroes and whites. *Journal of Marriage and the Family* 27: 200–203.

Brodsky, A. (1977). Countertransference issues and the woman therapist: Sex and the student therapist. *The Clinical Psychologist* 30(2): 12–14.

Brodsky, C. (1971). The pharmacotherapy system. *Psychosomatics* 11: 24–30.

Bronfenbrenner, U. (1961). Some familiar antecedents of responsibility and leadership in adolescents. In L. Petrullo and B. Bass (eds.), *Leadership and Interpersonal Behavior.* New York: Holt, 260.

Brooks, L. (1974). Interactive effects of sex and status on self-disclosure. *Journal of Counseling Psychology* 21:469–474.

______ (1978). Supermoms shift gears: Re-entry women. In L. Harmon, J. Birk, L. Fitzgerald, and M. Tanney (eds.), *Counseling Women.* Monterey: Brooks/Cole, 218–229.

Broverman, D., L. Klaiber, Y. Kabayashi, and W. Vogel (1968). Roles of activation and inhibition in sex differences in cognitive abilities. *Psychological Review* 75:23–50.

Broverman, I., D. Broverman, F. Clarkson, P. Rosenkrantz, and S. Vogel (1970). Sex-role stereotypes and clinical judgments of mental health. *Journal of Consulting and Clinical Psychology* 34:1–7.

Broverman, I., S. Vogel, D. Broverman, F. Clarkson, and P. Rosenkrantz (1972). Sex-role stereotypes: A current appraisal. *Journal of Social Issues* 28(2): 59–78.

Bryson, R., J. Bryson, M. Licht, and B. Licht (1976). The professional pair: Husband and wife psychologists. *American Psychologist* 31:10–16.

Buffery, A., and J. Gray (1972). Sex differences in the development of spatial and linguistic skills. In C. Ounsted and D. Taylor (eds.), *Gender Differences: Their Ontogeny and Significance.* Baltimore: William and Wilkins, 123–175.

Bugental, D., L. Love, and R. Gianetto (1971). Perfidious feminine faces. *Journal of Personality and Social Psychology* 17:314–318.

Burke, R., and T. Weir (1977). Husband-wife helping relationships: The mental hygiene function in marriage. *Psychological Reports* 40:911–925.

Burr, E., S. Dunn, and N. Farquhar (1972). Women and the language of inequality. *Social Education* 36:841–845.

Campbell, A. (1975). The American way of mating: Marriage sí, children only maybe. *Psychology Today* 8:37–43.

Campbell, D. Women deserve better (1973). *Personnel and Guidance Journal* 51:545–549.

Chandler, R. (1972). *Public Opinion: Changing Attitudes on Contemporary Political and Social Issues.* New York: Bowker.

Cherry, F., and K. Deaux (1975). Fear of success versus fear of gender-inconsistent behavior: A sex similarity. Paper presented at the Midwestern Psychological Association Meeting, Chicago.

Cherry L. (1975). Teacher-child verbal interaction: An approach to the study of sex differences. In B. Thorne and N. Henley (eds.), *Language and Sex: Difference and Dominance.* Rowley, Mass.: Newbury House, 172–183.

Cherry L., and M. Lewis (1976). Mothers and two-year-olds: A study of sex-differentiated aspects of verbal interaction. *Developmental Psychology* 12:278–282.

Chesler, P. (1971). Patient and patriarch: Women in the psychotherapeutic relationship. In V. Gornich and B. Moran (eds.), *Women in Sexist Society.* New York: Basic Books.

______ (1972). *Women and Madness.* New York: Doubleday.

______ (1973). A word about mental health and women. *Mental Hygiene* 37:5–7.

Collins, A., and W. Sedlacek (1972). Counselor ratings of male and female students. ERIC Document Reproduction Service, No. ED 071597.

Constantinople, A. (1973). Masculinity-feminity: An exception to a famous dictum? *Psychological Bulletin* 80:389–407.

Crandall, V. (1969). Sex differences in expectancy of intellectual and academic reinforcement. In C. Smith (ed.), *Achievement-Related Motives in Children.* New York: Russell Sage.

______ (1975). Sex differences in expectancy of intellectual and academic reinforcement. In R. Unger and F. Denmark (eds.), *Women: Dependent or Independent Variable?* New York: Psychological Dimensions, 650–685.

Crites, J. (1973). *Theory and Research Handbook, Career Maturity Inventory.* Monterey: CTB/McGraw-Hill.

Crowley, J., T. Levitin, and R. Quinn (1973). Seven deadly half-truths about women. *Psychology Today* 6:94–96.

Dailey, S. (1976). Big-time careers for the little woman: A dual-role dilemma. *Journal of Social Issues* 32(3): 85–98.

Deaux, K. (1976). *The Behavior of Women and Men.* Monterey, Calif.: Brooks/Cole.

Deaux, K., and T. Emswiller (1974). Explanations of successful performance on sex-linked tasks. *Journal of Personality and Social Psychology* 29:80–85.

Deaux, K., and E. Farris (1974). Attributing causes for one's performance: The effects of sex, norms, and outcome. Unpublished manuscript, Purdue University.

Deaux, K., and J. Taynor (1973). Evaluation of male and female ability: Bias works two ways. *Psychological Reports* 32:261–262.

Deaux, K., L. White, and E. Farris (1975). Skill versus luck: Field and laboratory studies of male and female preferences. *Journal of Personality and Social Psychology* 32(4): 629–636.

Deckard, B. (1975). *The Women's Movement: Political, Socioeconomic and Psychological Issues.* New York: Harper.

Dewey, C. (1977). Vocational counseling with women: A nonsexist technique. In E. Rawlings and D. Carter (eds.), *Psychotherapy for Women.* Springfield, Ill.: Charles C Thomas, 207–220.

Dobbs, J. (1972). Sex, setting and reactions to crowding on sidewalks. Paper presented at APA, Honolulu, August.

Douvan, E., and J. Adelson (1966). *The Adolescent Experience.* New York: Wiley.

Ebel, R. (1976). In defense of standardized testing. Paper presented at the Houghton-Mifflin Annual Measurement Conference, March, Iowa City, Iowa.

Eisenbud, R. (1977). Counter-transference issues in woman therapists: Value conflicts between woman therapists and women patients. *The Clinical Psychologist* 30(2): 14–17.

Ekstrom, R. (1972). Barriers to women's participation in post-secondary education: A review of the literature. In S. Ball and P. Cross, *Barriers to Women's Continuing Education.* A symposium presented at the American Psychological Association meeting, Honolulu, September.

Elliott, H. C. (1969). *Textbook of Neuroanatomy,* 2d ed. (1969). Philadelphia: Lippincott.

Ellis, A. (1974). The treatment of sex and love problems in women. In V. Franks and V. Burtle (eds.), *Women in Therapy.* New York: Brunner/Mazel, 284–306.

Entwistle, D. (1972). To dispel fantasies about fantasybased measures of achievement motivation. *Psychological Bulletin* 77:337–391.

Entwistle, D., and E. Greenberger (1970). *A Survey of Cognitive Styles in Maryland Ninth Graders: Views of Women's Roles.* Baltimore: Center for the Study of Social Organization of the Schools, Johns Hopkins University, November.

Epstein, C. (1973). Positive effects of the multiple negative: Explaining the success of black professional women. *American Journal of Sociology* 78: 912–935.

Exline, R., D. Gray, and D. Schuette (1965). Visual behavior in a dyad as affected by interview content and sex of respondent. *Journal of Personality and Social Psychology* 1:201–209.

Fabrikant, B. (1974). The psychotherapist and the female patient. In V. Franks and V. Burtle (eds.), *Women in Therapy*. New York: Brunner/Mazel.

Fasteau, M. (1974). *The Male Machine*. New York: McGraw-Hill.

Feather, N. (1969). Attribution of responsibility and valence of success and failure in relation to initial confidence and task performance. *Journal of Personality and Social Psychology* 13:129–144.

Feather, N., and J. Simon (1975). Reactions to male and female success and failure in sex-linked occupations: Impressions of personality, causal attributions, and perceived likelihood of different consequences. *Journal of Personality and Social Psychology* 31:20–31.

Feldman-Summers, S., and J. Kiesler (1974). Those who are number two try harder: The effects of sex on attributions of causality. *Journal of Personality and Social Psychology* 30:846–855.

Feshbach, S., and N. Feshback (1973). The young aggressors. *Psychology Today*, (April): 90–95.

Fidell, L. (1970). Empirical verification of sex discrimination in hiring practices in psychology. *American Psychologist* 25:1094–1097.

______ (1973). Put her down on drugs: Prescribed drug usage in women. Paper presented at the Western Psychological Association meeting, Anaheim, California, April.

Fish, S. (1975). A phenomenology of women. Unpublished doctoral dissertation, Southern Illinois University.

Fisher, J., E. O'Neal, and P. McDonald (1974). Female competitiveness as a function of a prior performance outcome, competitor's evaluation, and sex of competitor. Paper presented at the Midwestern Psychological Association meeting, Chicago.

Fishman, P. (1975). Study of male-female conversations. Paper presented at the American Sociological Association meeting, San Francisco, August.

Flaugher, R. (1974). *Bias in Testing: A Review and Discussion* (TM Report 36). Princeton, N.J.: ERIC Clearinghouse on Tests, Measurements, and Evaluation.

______ (1978). The many definitions of test bias. *American Psychologist* 33(7): 671–679.

Ford, D. (1978). Counseling for the strengths of the black woman. In L. Harmon, J. Birk, L. Fitzgerald, and M. Tanney (eds), *Counseling Women*. Monterey: Brooks/Cole, 186–192.

Forisha, B. (1976). Creativity and mental imagery in men and women: Unpublished manuscript.

_____ (1978). *Sex-Roles and Personal Awareness.* Morristown, N.J.: General Learning Press.

Frank, J. (1961). *Persuasion and Healing.* Baltimore: The Johns Hopkins Press.

Frazier, N., and M. Sadker (1973). *Sexism in School and Society.* New York: Harper.

Freeman, J. (1971). The social construction of the second sex. In M. Barskof, (ed.), *Roles Women Play.* Belmont, Calif.: Brooks/Cole.

Friedrick, L. (1976). Achievement motivation in college women revisited: Implications for women, men, and the gathering of coconuts. *Sex Roles* 2(1): 47–61.

Frieze, I. and S. Ramsey (1976). Nonverbal maintenance of traditional sex roles. *Journal of Social Issues* 32(3): 133–141.

Garai, J. (1970). Sex differences in mental health. *Genetic Psychology Monographs* 81:123–142.

Garske, J. (1975). Motive to avoid success, sensitivity to rejection and male feedback as determinant of female performance in a cross-sexed competition. Paper presented at the Eastern Psychological Association meeting, New York, April.

_____ (1975). Role variation as a determinant of attributed masculinity and feminity. *The Journal of Psychology* 91:31–37.

Gerbner, G., and L. Gross (1976). The scary world of TV's heavy viewer. *Psychology Today* 9:41–45.

Gettleman, S., and J. Markowitz (1974). *The Courage to Divorce.* New York: Simon and Schuster.

Gillespie, D. (1971). Who has the power? The marital struggle. *Journal of Marriage and the Family* 33:445–458.

Gillis, J. (1974). Social influence therapy: the therapist as manipulator. *Psychology Today* 8:91.

Glick, P. (1975). A demographer looks at American families. *Journal of Marriage and the Family* 37:15–26.

Goldberg, P. (1968). Are women prejudiced against women? *Transaction* 5: 28–30.

Goldburg, S., and M. Lewis (1969). Play behavior in the year-old infant: Early sex differences. *Child Development* 40:21–30.

Golub, S. (1973). The effect of premenstrual depression and anxiety on personality and cognitive function. Unpublished doctoral dissertation, Fordham University.

Gove, W. The relationship between sex roles, mental illness, and marital status. *Social Forces* 51:34–44.

Gove, W., and J. Tudor (1973). Adult sex roles and mental illness. *American Journal of Sociology* 78:812–835.

Gulliksen, H. (1976). When high validity may indicate a faulty criterion (RM 76-10). Princeton, N.J.: Educational Testing Service.

Gurwitz, S., and K. Dodge (1975). Adults' evaluations of a child as a function of sex of adult and sex of child. *Journal of Personality and Social Psychology* 32(5): 822–828.

Guterman, S. (1972). *Black Psyche.* Berkeley: The Glendessary Press.

Gutmann, D. (1970). Female ego styles and generational conflict. In J. Bardwick, E. Douvan, M. Horner, and D. Gutmann (eds.), *Feminine Personality and Conflict.* Brooks/Cole.

Guzell, M. (1977). Problems of personal change in women's studies courses. In E. Rawlings and D. Carter (eds.), *Psychotherapy for Women.* Springfield, Ill.: Charles C. Thomas, 310–327.

Halleck, S. (1971). Therapy is the handmaiden of the status quo. *Psychology Today* 4:30.

Hare-Mustin, R. (1977). Courage to look within: A discussants view of countertransference. *The Clinical Psychologist* 30(2): 17–22.

Harmon, L. (1973). Sexual bias in interest measurement. *Measurement and Evaluation in Guidance* 5:496–501.

______ (1977). Career counseling for women. In E. Rawlings and D. Carter (eds.), *Psychotherapy for Women.* Springfield, Ill.: Charles C Thomas, 197–206.

Hartnagel, T. (1970). Father absence and self-conception among low class white and negro boys. *Social Problems* 18:152–163.

Haskell, M. (1973). *From Reverence to Rape: The Treatment of Women in the Movies.* Baltimore: Penguin.

Hawkins, R., and S. Pingree (1978). Effects of changing proportions of the sexes on ratings of occupational prestige. *Psychology of Women Quarterly* 2(4): 314–322.

Heider, F. (1958). *The Psychology of Interpersonal Relations.* New York: Wiley.

Heim, A. (1970). *Intelligence and Personality.* New York: Penguin.

Helmreich, R., and J. Stapp (1974). Short forms of the Texas Social Behavior Inventory. *Bulletin of the Psychonomic Society* 4: 473–475.

Helms, J., and J. Simons (1975). Age and sex of counselor as components of perceived counselor credibility. Unpublished manuscript, Washington State University.

Henley, N. (1973). The politics of touch. In P. Brown (ed.), *Radical Psychology*. New York: Harper, 421–433.

Hennig, M., and A. Jardin (1977). *The Managerial Woman*. New York: Anchor/Doubleday.

Hermans, H., J. ter Laak, and P. Maes (1972). Achievement motivation and fear of failure in family and school. *Developmental Psychology* 6: 520–528.

Hill, C. (1975). Sex of client and sex and experience level of counselor. *Journal of Counseling Psychology* 22:6–11.

Hite, S. (1976). *The Hite Report: A Nationwide Survey on Female Sexuality*. New York: Macmillan.

Hoffman, L. (1972). Early childhood experiences and woman's achievement motives. *Journal of Social Issues* 28(2): 129–156.

______ (1974). Effects of maternal employment on the child: A review of the research. *Developmental Psychology* 10(2): 204–228.

______ (1977). Changes in family roles, socialization and sex differences. *American Psychologist* 32(8): 644–657.

Hoffman, L., and F. Nye (1974). *Working Mothers*. San Francisco: Jossey-Bass.

Holland, J. (1966). *The Psychology of Vocational Choice*. Waltham, Mass.: Blaisdell.

______ (1974). The use and evaluation of interest inventories and simultations. Center for Social Organization of Schools. (ERIC Document Reproduction Service, No. ED 092 568).

Holland, J., and D. Whitney (1968). *Changes In the Vocational Plans of College Students: Orderly or Random?* Iowa City: American College Testing Program, April.

Hollingworth, L. (1914). Variability as related to sex differences in achievement. *American Journal of Sociology* 19:510–530.

______ (1916). Social devices for impelling women to bear and rear children. *American Journal of Sociology* 22:19–29.

Horner, M. Sex differences in achievement motivation and performance in competitive and noncompetitive situations. Unpublished doctoral dissertation, University of Michigan.

______ (1972). Toward an understanding of achievement-related conflict in women. *Journal of Social Issues* 28(2): 157–175.

Hough, K., and B. Allen (1975). Is the women's movement erasing the mark of oppression from the female psyche? *Journal of Psychology* 89: 249–258.

Howell, M. (1974). What medical schools teach about women. *New England Journal of Medicine* 291:304–307.

Huarte, J. (1959). *The Examination of Mens Wits* (trans. R. Carew). Gainesville, Fla.: Scholars' Facsimiles and Reprints.

Hunt, J., and L. Hunt (1977). Dilemmas and contradictions of status: The case of the dual-career family. *Social Problems* 24(4): 407–416.

Hutt, C. (1972). *Males and Females.* Middlesex, England: Penguin.

Jackson, D. (1978). *The Jackson Vocational Interest Survey.* Port Huron, Mich.: Research Psychologists Press.

Jackson, D., S. Ahmed, and N. Heapy (1976). Is achievement motivation a unitary construct? *Journal of Research in Personality* 10:1–21.

Jackson, J. (1973). Family organization and technology. In K. Miller and R. Dreger (eds.), *Comparative Studies of Blacks and Whites in the United States.* New York: Seminar Press.

Jakubowski, P. (1977). Assertive behavior and clinical problems of women: Self-assertion training procedures for women. In E. Rawlings and D. Carter (eds.), *Psychotherapy for Women.* Springfield, Ill.: Charles C Thomas, 147–190.

______ (1978). Facilitating the growth of women through assertive training. *The Counseling Psychologist* 4:75 and in L. Harmon, J. Birk, L. Fitzgerald, and M. Tanney (eds.), *Counseling Women.* Monterey, Calif.: Brooks/Cole, 106–122.

Jellison, J., R. Jackson-White, and R. Bruder (1974). Fear of success? A situational approach. Paper presented at the Western Psychological Association Meeting, San Francisco.

Jennings, S. (1975). Effects of sex typing in children's stories on preference and recall. *Child Development* 46(1): 220–223.

Kagan, J. (1975). The emergence of sex differences. In F. Rebelsky (ed.), *Life: The Continuous Process.* New York: Knopf.

Kaley, M. (1971). Attitudes toward the dual role of the married professional woman. *American Psychologist* 26:301–306.

Kanter, R. (1976a). Why bosses turn bitchy. *Psychology Today* 9:56–59.

______ (1976b). Women in organizations: Sex roles, group dynamics, and change strategies. In A. Sargent (ed.), *Beyond Sex Roles.* St. Paul: West Publishing, 371–387.

Kardener, S., M. Fuller, and I. Mensh (1973). A survey of physicians' attitudes and practices regarding erotic and nonerotic contact with patients. *American Journal of Psychiatry* 130:1077–1081.

Kaschak, E. (1976). Cited in sexist ratings. *Human Behavior* 5:50.

Katz, M. (1973). Female motive to avoid success: A psychological barrier or a response to deviancy? Unpublished manuscript. Educational Testing Service, Princeton, N.J.

Keller, S. (1974). The female role: Constants and change. In V. Franks and V. Burtle (eds.), *Women In Therapy*. New York: Brunner/Mazel, 411–434.

Kelly, J., and L. Worell (1976). Parent behaviors related to masculine, feminine, and androgynous sex role orientations. *Journal of Consulting and Clinical Psychology* 44:843–851.

King, M. (1973). The politics of sexual stereotypes. *The Black Scholar* 4: 12–23.

Kipnis, D. (1974). Inner direction, other direction, and achievement motivation. *Human Development* 17(5): 321–343.

Kirk, W. (1975). Where are you? Black mental health model. *Journal of Non-White Concerns* 3:177–188.

Knefelkamp, L., C. Widick, and B. Stroad (1978). Cognitive-developmental theory: A guide to counseling women. In L. Harmon, J. Birk, L. Fitzgerald, and M. Tanny (eds.), *Counseling Women*. Monterey, Calif.: Brooks/Cole, 173–185.

Koenigsknecht, R., and P. Friedman (1976). Syntax development in boys and girls. *Child Development* 47(4): 1109–1115.

Kohn, M., and C. Schooler (1973). Occupational experience and psychological functioning: An assessment of reciprocal effects. *American Sociological Review* 38:97–118.

Ladner, J. (1971). *Tomorrow's Tomorrow: The Black Woman*. Garden City, N.Y.: Doubleday.

Lakoff, R. (1975). *Language and Woman's Place*. New York: Harper.

Landsell, H. (1976). The use of factor scores from the Wechsler-Bellevue Scale of Intelligence in assessing patients with temporal lobe removals. *Cortex* 4:257–268.

Lao, R., W. Upchurch, B. Corwin, and W. Grossnickle (1975). Biased attitudes toward females as indicated by ratings of intelligence and likeability. *Psychological Reports* 37:1315–1320.

Leventhal, G., and J. Michaels (1971). Locus of cause and equity motivation as determinants of reward allocation. *Journal of Personality and Social Psychology* 17:229–235.

Lewis, M. (1972). Culture and gender roles: There's no unisex in the nursery. *Psychology Today* 5:54–57.

Lewis, M., and R. Freedle (1973). Mother-infant dyad: The cradle of meaning. In P. Pliner, L. Kramer, and T. Alloway (eds.), *Communication and Affect: Language and Thought.* New York: Academic Press.

Libby, W., and D. Yaklevich (1973). Personality determinants of eye contact and direction of gaze aversion. *Journal of Personality and Social Psychology* 27:197–206.

Linn, L. (1971). Physician characteristics and attitudes toward legitimate use of psychotherapeutic drugs. *Journal of Health and Social Behavior* 12: 132–140.

Lipman-Blumen, J., and H. Leavitt (1976). Vicarious and direct achievement patterns in adulthood. *The Counseling Psychologist* 6:26–32.

Maccoby, E. (1966). Sex differences in intellectual functioning. In E. Maccoby (ed.), *The Development of Sex Differences.* Stanford, Calif.: Stanford University Press, 25–55.

Maccoby, E., and C. Jacklin (1974). *The Psychology of Sex Differences.* Stanford, Calif.: Stanford University Press.

Makosky, V. (1972). Fear of success, sex-role orientation of the task and competitive conditions as variables affecting women's performance in achievement-oriented situations. Paper presented at the Midwestern Psychological Association Meeting, Cleveland, May.

Malina, R. (1973). Biological substrata. In K. Miller and R. Dreger (eds.), *Comparative Studies of Blacks and Whites in the United States.* New York: Seminar Press.

Maslow, A. (1970). *Motivation and Personality,* 2d ed. New York: Harper.

Masters, W., and V. Johnson (1975). *The Pleasure Bond: A New Look at Sexuality and Commitment.* Boston: Little, Brown.

Maxfield, R. B. (1976). Sex-role stereotypes of psychotherapists. Unpublished doctoral dissertation, Adelphi University.

McCarthy, M. (1973). An exploration into the measured work values of counselors. Unpublished doctoral dissertation, Boston College.

McClelland, D. (1964). *The Achieving Society.* New York: Free Press.

McClelland, D., J. Atkinson, R. Clark, and E. Lowell (1953). *The Achievement Motive.* New York: Appleton-Century-Crofts.

McEwen, M. (1975). Counseling women: A review of the research. *Journal of College Student Personnel* 16:382–388.

McGlone, J. (1976). Sex differences in functional brain asymmetry. *Research Bulletin No. 378,* University of Western Ontario.

McMillin, M. (1972). Attitudes of college men toward involvement of married women. *Vocational Guidance Quarterly* 21:8–11.

Meerdink, G., and P. Schmitt (1977). The effect of androgyny on attribution of causality. Unpublished manuscript, University of Toledo.

Mehrabian, A. (1972). *Nonverbal Communication.* Chicago: Aldine-Atherton.

Mellon, J. (1973). *Women and Their Sexuality In the New Film.* New York: Dell.

Meyer, J., and B. Sobieszek (1972). Effect of a child's sex on adult interpretations of its behavior. *Developmental Psychology* 6:42–48.

Meyer, R., and R. Lewis (1976). New wine from old wineskins: Marital power research. *Journal of Comparative Family Studies* 7(3): 397–407.

Mickish, G. (1971). Can women function as successfully as men in the role of elementary principal? *Research Reports on Educational Administration* 2(4) (ERIC Document Reproduction Service, ED 062 679).

Mill, J. (1955). *The Subjection of Women.* London: Dent.

Miller, S. (1975). Effects of maternal employment on sex role perception, interests, and self-esteem in kindergarten girls. *Developmental Psychology* 11:405–406.

Mitchell, J. (1974). *Psychoanalysis and Feminism.* New York: Pantheon.

Monahan, L., D. Kuhn, and P. Shaver (1974). Intrapsychic versus cultural explanations of the "fear of success" motive. *Journal of Personality and Social Psychology* 29:60–64.

Money, J., and A. Ehrhardt (1972). *Man and Woman, Boy and Girl.* Baltimore: The John Hopkins Press.

Moss, H. (1967). Sex, age, and state as determinants of mother-infant interaction. *Merrill-Palmer Quarterly* 13(1): 19–36.

Murray, P. (1970). The liberation of black women. In M. Thompson (ed.), *Voices of the New Feminism.* Boston: Beacon.

Naditch, S. (1976). Experimental demand characteristics and sex differences on the rod and frame test. Paper presented at the Annual Convention of the American Psychological Association, Washington, D.C., September.

National Disease and Therapeutic Index (1970). *Annual Report.* Amber, Pa.: Lea.

Nelson, H., and P. Goldman (1969). Attitudes of high school students and young adults toward the gainful employment of married women. *The Family Coordinator* 18:251–255.

Nevill, D., and S. Damico (1977). Developmental components of role conflict in women. *Journal of Psychology* 95:195–198.

NOW. (1978). *A Consumer's Guide to Nonsexist Therapy.* New York: National Organization for Women.

O'Leary, V. (1974). Some attitudinal barriers to occupational aspirations in women. *Psychological Bulletin* 81:809–826.

______ (1977). *Toward Understanding Women.* Monterey, Calif.: Brooks/Cole.

O'Leary, V., and C. Depner (1975). College males' ideal female: Changes in sex-role stereotypes. *Journal of Social Psychology* 95:139–140.

Oliver, L. (1975). Counseling implications of recent research on women. *Personnel and Guidance Journal* 53:430–437.

Oppedisano-Reich, M. (1976). The effect of a patient's social class, race, and sex on mental health professionals' diagnoses, prognoses, and recommendations for treatment. Unpublished doctoral dissertation, Adelphi University.

Osen, L. (1974). *Women In Mathematics.* Cambridge: The MIT Press.

Osipow, S. (1968). *Theories of Career Development.* New York: Appleton-Century-Crofts.

Osmond, M., and P. Martin (1975). Sex and sexism: A comparison of male and female sex-role attitudes. *Journal of Marriage and the Family* 37: 744–758.

Parelius, A. (1975). Emerging sex-role attitudes, expectations and strains among college women. *Journal of Marriage and the Family* 37:146–153.

Parlee, M. (1972). Comments on "Roles of activation and inhibition in sex differences in cognitive abilities" by Broverman et. al. *Psychological Review* 79:180–184.

Pedersen, D., M. Shinedling, and D. Johnson (1975). Effects of sex of examiner and subject on children's quantitative test performance. In R. Unger and F. Denmark (eds.), *Women: Dependent or Independent Variable*? New York: *Psychological Dimensions,* 410–416.

Pedersen, F., and K. Robson (1969). Father participation in infancy. *American Journal of Orthopsychiatry* 39(3): 466–472.

Pendergrass, V. (1974). Women as clinicians in private practice. *American Psychologist* 29:533–535.

Petersen, A. (1976). Physical androgyny and cognitive functioning in adolescence. *Developmental Psychology* 12(6): 524–533.

Peterson, C., and J. Peterson (1973). Preferences for sex of offspring as a measure of change in sex attitudes. *Psychology* 10:3–5.

Pheterson, G., S. Kiesler, and P. Goldberg (1971). Evaluation of the performance of women as a function of their sex, achievement, and personal history. *Journal of Personality and Social Psychology* 19:114–118.

Pietropinto, A., and J. Simenauer (1977). *Beyond the Male Myth.* New York: Times Books.

Pleck, J. (1976). The male sex role: Definitions, problems, and sources of change. *Journal of Social Issues* 32(3): 155–164.

______ (1977). The work-family role system. *Social Problems* 24(4): 417–427.

Pohlman, E. (1969). *The Psychology of Birth Planning:* Cambridge, Mass.: Schenkman.

Poloma, M., and T. Garland (1971). The married professional woman: A study in the tolerance of domestication. *Journal of Marriage and the Family* 33:531–540.

Prather, J., and L. Fidell (1972). Put her down and drug her up. Paper presented at the American Sociological Association meeting, New Orleans, August.

Psathas, C. (1968). Toward a theory of occupational choice for women. *Sociology and Social Research* 52:253–268.

Raph, J., M. Goldberg, and A. Passow (1966). *Bright Underachievers.* New York: Teacher's College Press.

Rawlings, E., and D. Carter (eds.) (1977). *Psychotherapy for Women.* Springfield, Ill.: Charles C Thomas.

Rebelsky, F., and C. Hanks (1971). Fathers' verbal interaction with infants in the first three months of life. *Child Development* 42:63–68.

Rheingold, H., and K. Cook (1975). The content of boys' and girls' rooms as an index of parents' behavior. *Child Development* 46(2): 459–463.

Rice, J., and D. Rice (1973). Implications of the women's liberation movement for psychotherapy. *American Journal of Psychiatry* 130:191–196.

______ (1977). Non-sexist marital therapy. *Journal of Marriage and Family Counseling* 3: 3–10.

Rosen, B., B. Locke, I. Goldberg, and H. Babigian (1972). Identification of emotional disturbance in patients seen in general medical clinics. *Hospital and Community Psychiatry* 23(12): 364–370.

Rosenberg, M. (1972). Race, ethnicity and self-esteem. In S. Guterman (ed.), *Black Psyche.* Berkeley: The Glendessary Press, 87–99.

Rosenkrantz, P., S. Vogel, H. Bee, I. Broverman, and D. Broverman (1968). Sex-role stereotypes and self-concepts in college students. *Journal of Consulting and Clinical Psychology* 32:287–295.

Rothbart, M., and E. Maccoby (1966). Parents' differential reactions to sons and daughters. *Journal of Personality and Social Psychology* 4: 237–243.

Rubin, J., F. Provenzano, and Z. Luria (1974). The eye of the beholder: Parents' views on sex of newborns. *American Journal of Orthopsychiatry* 44(4): 512–519.

Rubovits, P. (1975). Early experience and the achieving orientations of American middle-class girls. In M. Maehr and W. Stallings (eds.), *Culture, Child and School.* Monterey, Calif.: Brooks/Cole.

Saretsky, L. (1977). Sex related countertransference: Issues of a female therapist. *The Clinical Psychologist* 30(2): 11–12.

Scanzoni, J. (1975). Sex roles, economic factors, and marital solidarity in black and white marriages. *Journal of Marriage and the Family* 37(1): 130–144.

______ (1975). *Sex Roles, Lifestyles and Childbearing: Changing Patterns in Marriage and the Family.* New York: Free Press.

Schaffer, K. (1976). Evaluating job satisfaction and success for emotionally maladjusted men. *Journal of Vocational Behavior* 9:329–335.

Schlesinger, A. (1966). An informal history of love, USA. *The Saturday Evening Post* 239(4): 30–32.

Schlossberg, N., and J. Goodman (1972). Revision of the Strong Vocational Interest Blanks. Resolution to the American Personnel and Guidance Association, March 29.

Schlossberg, N., and J. Pietrofesa (1978). Perspectives on counseling bias: Implications for counselor education. In L. Harmon, J. Birk, L. Fitzgerald, and M. Tanny (eds.), *Counseling Women.* Monterey, Calif.: Brooks/Cole, 59–74.

Seidenberg, R. (1977). Should this marriage (counseling) be saved? In E. Rawlings and D. Carter (eds.), *Psychotherapy for Women.* Springfield, Ill.: Charles C Thomas, 128–142.

Serbin, L., and K. O'Leary (1975). How nursery schools teach girls to shut up. *Psychology Today* 9:56–58.

Shaffer, D., and C. Wegley (1974). Success orientation and sex-role congruence as determinents of the attractiveness of competent women. *Journal of Personality* 42:586–600.

Sherman, J. (1971). *On the Psychology of Women: A Survey of Empirical Studies.* Springfield, Ill.: Charles C Thomas.

______ (1974). Field articulation, sex, spatial visualization, dependency, practice, laterality of the brain, and birth order. *Perceptual and Motor Skills* 38:1223–1235.

Sherman, J., C. Koufacos, and J. Kenworthy (1978). Therapists: Their attitudes and information about women. *Psychology of Women Quarterly* 2(4): 299–313.

Shields, S. (1974). The variability hypothesis and sex differences in intelligence. Unpublished manuscript, Pennsylvania State University.

______ (1975). Functionalism, Darwinism, and the psychology of women: A study in social myth. *American Psychologist* 30(7): 739–754.

Silverstein, B., and R. Krate (1975). *Children of the Dark Ghetto.* New York: Prager.

Simons, J., and J. Helms (1976). Influence of counselors' marital status, sex, and age on college and noncollege women's counselor preferences. *Journal of Counseling Psychology* 23(4): 380–386.

Siskel, F. (1976). Cited in The beauty bias. *Human Behavior* (5):51.

Smith, W., A. Burlew, M. Mosley, and W. M. Whitney (1978). *Minority Issues In Mental Health.* Reading, Mass.: Addison-Wesley.

Spence, J., and R. Helmreich (1972). The Attitudes Toward Women Scale. JSAS *Catalog of Selected Documents in Psychology* 2:66.

______ (1978). *Masculinity and Femininity.* Austin: University of Texas Press.

Spence, J., R. Helmreich, and J. Stapp (1973). A short version of the Attitudes Toward Women Scale. *Bulletin of the Psychonomic Society* 2: 219–220.

______ (1974). The Personal Attributes Questionnaire. JSAS *Catalog of Selected Documents in Psychology* 4:127.

______ (1975). Ratings of self and peers on sex-role attributes and their relation to self-esteem and conceptions of masculinity and femininity. *Journal of Personality and Social Psychology* 32:29–39.

Stake, J. (1976). The effect of information regarding group performance norms on goal setting in males and females. *Sex Roles* 2(1): 23–28.

Stein, A., and M. Bailey (1973). The socialization of achievement orientation in females. *Psychological Bulletin* 80(5): 345–366.

Stein, L., A. Del Gaudio, and M. Ansley (1976). A comparison of female and male neurotic depressives. *Journal of Clinical Psychology* 32(1): 19–21.

Stein, L., M. Fox, and D. Luepnitz (1974). Therapists' judgments of prognosis, severity of disturbance, and treatment needs as a function of patients' sex. Unpublished manuscript, University of Rochester.

Steinmann, A. (1975). Sex roles: Twenty years of cross-cultural research. Paper presented at American Psychological Association Meeting, Chicago, September.

Steinmann, A., and P. Fox (1970). Attitudes toward women's family role among black and white undergraduates. *The Family Coordinator* 19: 363–367.

Sternglanz, S., and L. Serbin (1974). Sex role stereotyping in children's television programs. *Developmental Psychology* 10: 710–715.

Stoller, R. (1968). *Sex and Gender.* New York: Science House.

Stricker, G. (1977). Implications of research for psychotherapeutic treatment of women. *American Psychologist* 32(1): 14–22.

Super, D. (1957). *The Psychology of Careers.* New York: Harper.

______ (1972). Vocational development theory: Persons, positions and processes. In J. Whitely and H. Resnikoff (eds.), *Perspectives On Vocational Development.* Washington, D.C.: American Personnel and Guidance Association, 13–33.

Tavris, C. (1973). Who likes women's liberation—and why: The case of the unliberated liberals. *Journal of Social Issues* 29(4): 175–198.

Tavris, C., and C. Offir (1977). *The Longest War: Sex Differences In Perspective.* New York: Harcourt.

Taynor, J., and K. Deaux (1973). When women are more deserving than men: Equity, attribution, and perceived sex differences. *Journal of Personality and Social Psychology* 28:360–367.

Terman, L., and M. Oden (1947, 1959). *Genetic Studies of Genius,* Vol. 4 and Vol. 5. Stanford: Stanford University Press.

Thomas, A., and N. Stewart (1971). Counselor response to female clients with deviate and conforming career goals. *Journal of Counseling Psychology* 18:352–357.

Thorndike, E. (1914). *Educational Psychology Briefer Course.* New York: Teachers College, Columbia University.

Tittle, C. (1974). Sex bias in educational measurement: Fact or fiction? *Measurement and Evaluation in Guidance* 6:219–226.

Tobias, S. (1976). Math anxiety: Why is a smart girl like you counting on her fingers? *Ms* 5:56–59.

Touhey, J. (1974a). Effects of additional women professionals on ratings of occupational prestige and desirability. *Journal of Personality and Social Psychology* 29:86–89.

______ (1974b). Effects of additional men on prestige and desirability of occupations typically performed by women. *Journal of Applied Social Psychology* 4(4): 330–335.

Tressemer, D. (1974). Fear of success: Popular but unproven. *Psychology Today* 7(10): 82–85.

Turner, B. (1972). Socialization and career orientation among black and white college women. Paper presented at the American Psychological Association meeting, Honolulu, September.

Unger, R., and F. Denmark (1975). *Women: Dependent or Independent Variable*? New York: Psychological Dimensions.

United States Department of Labor (1974). *Monthly Labor Review*. April.

Vanek, J. (1974). Time spent in housework. *Scientific American* 231: 116–120.

Veroff, J., L. McClelland, and D. Ruhland (1975). Varieties of achievement motivation. In M. Mednick, S. Tangri, and L. Hoffman (eds.), *Women and Achievement*. New York: Wiley, 172–205.

Waber, D. (1976). Sex differences in cognition: A function of maturation rate? *Science* 192:572–574.

Walker, K. (1973). Effect of family characteristics on time contributed for household work by various members. Paper presented at the American Home Economics Association meeting, Atlantic City.

Watson, J. (1926). Studies on the growth of the emotions. *Psychologies of 1925*. Worcester, Mass.: Clark University Press.

Wechsler, D. (1958). *The Measurement and Appraisal of Adult Intelligence*, 4th ed. Baltimore: Williams and Wilkins.

Weiner, B. (1972). *Theories of Motivation*. New York: Markham.

Weitz, S. (1977). *Sex Roles*. New York: Oxford University Press.

Weitzman, L. (1975). Sex-role socialization. In J. Freeman (ed.), *Women: A Feminist Perspective*. Palo Alto: Mayfield, 105–144.

Williams, E. (1976). *Notes of a Feminist Therapist*. New York: Praeger.

Williams, J. (1977). *Psychology of Women: Behavior In a Biosocial Context*. New York: Norton.

Wirtenberg, T., and C. Nakamura (1976). Education: Barrier or boon to changing occupational roles of women? *Journal of Social Issues* 32(3): 165–179.

Wolfson, K. (1972). Career development of college women. Unpublished doctoral dissertation, University of Minnesota.

Women on Words and Images (1972). Dick and Jane as victims: Sex stereotyping on prime time TV. Princeton, N.J.

Women on Words and Images (1975). Channeling children: Sex stereotyping on prime time TV. Princeton, N.J.

Women's Bureau, U.S. Department of Labor (1971). *Women Workers Today.* Washington, D.C.: Women's Bureau.

______ (1972). *Twenty Facts on Women Workers.* Washington, D.C.: Women's Bureau.

______ (1976). *Women Workers Today.* Washington, D.C.: Women's Bureau.

Zanna, M. and S. Pack (1975). On the self-fulfilling nature of apparent sex differences in behavior. *Journal of Experimental Social Psychology* 11: 583–591.

Zimmerman, D., and C. West (1975). Sex roles, interruptions and silences in conversation. In B. Thorne and N. Henley (eds.), *Language and Sex: Difference and Dominance.* Rowley, Mass.: Newbury House, 105–129.

Zuckerman, M., and L. Wheeler (1975). To dispel fantasies about the fantasy-based measure of fear of success. *Psychological Bulletin* 82(6): 932–946.

Zytowski, D. (1969). Toward a theory of career development for women. *Personnel and Guidance Journal* 47:660–664.

Index